MW00571366

Director's Cut

# DAVID SOLWAY

# DIRECTOR'S CUT

The Porcupine's Quill

National Library of Canada Cataloguing in Publication Data

Solway, David, 1941–
Director's Cut

ISBN 0-88984-272-8

1. Canadian poetry (English) – 20th century – History and criticism
2. Poets, Canadian
I. Title.

PS8143.S66 2003      c811'.5409      2003-905141-2

1   2   3   •   05   04   03

Published by The Porcupine's Quill
68 Main Street, Erin, Ontario NOB 1TO
www.sentex.net/~pql

Readied for the press by John Metcalf; copy edited by Doris Cowan.

Represented in Canada by the Literary Press Group.
Trade orders are available from University of Toronto Press.

We acknowledge the support of the Ontario Arts Council,
and the Canada Council for the Arts for our publishing program.
The financial support of the Government of Canada
through the Book Publishing Industry Development Program
is also gratefully acknowledged. Thanks, also, to the Government
of Ontario through the Ontario Media Development Corporation's
Ontario Book Initiative.

Canada Council
for the Arts

Conseil des Arts
du Canada

ONTARIO ARTS COUNCIL
CONSEIL DES ARTS DE L'ONTARIO

Canadä

# TABLE OF CONTENTS

*For the members of the Jubilate Circle*

But always words waste from inward out
And I who was fastened to that furious choice
Turned out to hear myself as a contrary shout.
            – W. S. Graham, 'As Brilliance Fell'

Be fierce and unrelenting in the hunt, for the quarry
is clever and resilient.
            – Sinperlavio Ivo, *Diaries of a Tracker*

# PREFACE

AFTER WORKING THEIR WAY through this collection of essays, articles and reviews (with a few exceptions), readers may be forgiven for thinking they have encountered a hometown Savonarola committing most of contemporary Canadian literature to the bonfire of the inanities. Or closer to our own tradition, say a local version of Captain Hercules Vinegar of Hockley in the Hole, Fielding's pseudonym in *The Champion* of 1740. (Certainly, I would hope, not a poetic clone of B. R. Myers promulgating another *Reader's Manifesto*.) I admit much of what I have written here reads like a critical auto-da-fé or a script for a crusading literary polemic against all and sundry, and that the tone is often relentless and lurid. Nevertheless, I sense that the time has arrived to take stock and engage passionately if our literature, and especially our poetry, is ever to be rescued from the swamp of second-rateness into which it has so complaisantly descended. I am not mincing words here. I am convinced that almost all of the poetry (and much of the fiction) being written in Canada these days – with only a couple of redeeming exceptions that stand out like crop circles in a featureless plain – is turgid, spurious and pedestrian stuff, the lame result of two highly questionable developments: (1) the proliferation of creative writing departments, those factories of undeviating blandness, in universities throughout the country, and (2) a largely subsidized literature industry, abetted by a press of cousinly critics and reviewers, intended to construct a patchwork national psyche, create a sense of ideological cohesion and glorify the tribe. (Hence, also, the growing multicultural circus – the many as facets of the nebulous one – which, as Matt Cohen warns in *Typing: A life in 26 keys*, is transforming Canadian culture 'into a mosaic of ethnic folk dances to be celebrated by a few people with long memories after they've had a few drinks.') I will argue throughout that in consequence of this we have sponsored a coterie of underachieving overproducers and colluded in their diffusion by virtue of our silent complicity or our chauvinism.

That is why I am ready to challenge the literary hegemony of what we might call the Big Four – Al Purdy, Margaret Atwood, Michael Ondaatje and Anne Carson – all of whom I contend are writers of such inferior quality that in a truly literate society they would be recognized as a national embarrassment. The same evaluation applies to the little infinite of fellow travellers – some of whom I coffin within – who populate the journals, reading circuits, chat rooms, granting corridors and minority festivals like that group of subordinate settlers in the district of Nox that John Galt writes about in *Bogle Corbet*. But though I have been able to mention only a limited number of these Noxians, their names carry metonymic importance, being readily interchangeable with those I have not had the space to deal with adequately.

Generally speaking, although many readers, and particularly those among the younger generation of students and writers, are growing heartily tired of this galaxy of plodders breveted above their proper rank, we are on the whole far too nice, too politically correct and, in a word, too 'Canadian' to register our disapproval bluntly and agonistically. The last thing we want to do is offend anyone. Or if we do feel uneasy with the calibre of current production, we tend to respond with the throwaway irony of a brief remark that signals a safety-first intelligence or in the calm and measured tones of assumed effectiveness. All that such manoeuvres ensure is that nothing changes while conscience is appeased. To complicate matters even more, I suspect that we are mostly incapable of acknowledging true excellence, or if we do come across its rare presence and perceive it for what it is, we are prone to retreat in fear and resentment before that which indicts our habitual incompetence. Further, those of us who are implicated in the writing community have little desire to jeopardize our chances at benefiting from a reasonably lucrative prize and granting lottery, which is to a large extent controlled by the players themselves.

Another question that needs to be addressed has to do with the international acclaim accorded some of these writers, in particular Atwood, Ondaatje and Carson, whether as novelists or poets or both. How is it possible that a drone, an entrepreneur and a cipher respectively could be so fêted and lionized in the foreign press and that a veritable horde of scantlings should receive hospitality in their wake? Domestic honours may always be explained or explained away but a welcome reception abroad seems puzzling. I would argue that what we are seeing here is largely the result of a phenomenon well known to anthropologists, namely, the increasing scarcity of 'field cultures', owing to the fact that they have either been wiped off the map or have already been 'done', and thoroughly at that. What anthropologist studies Samoa these days? Who cares about the Bororo or Nambikwara now? (Indeed, so impoverished has the discipline become that anthropologists now tend to study other anthropologists, investigating Mead and deconstructing Lévi-Strauss rather than camping in the vanishing outback.) But let a ragtag society of hunters and gatherers be discovered in some nearly inaccessible region of the Siberian taiga and it will soon be swarmed, analysed, documented, filmed and endlessly discussed by a mob of Guggenheims, Fulbrights and Shirks. The syndrome at work here is that of the hungry ethnologist looking for a people to write up and a caste of shamans to interview, classify and archive in order to avoid the barren reaches of both theoretical self-absorption and palpable unemployment.

In the same way, Canlit is one of the last outposts of literary discovery still available to cultural scavengers who need a subject for a dissertation or depend on government handouts to endow another Department of Canadian Studies and fund the growing round of conferences on even the most obscure and antiquated of backwoods female dilettantes. We have become *exotic*, one of the great ironies of current literary study, though the occasional observer remains baffled by the phenomenon. I recall Professor Kurt Müller of the University of Jena, quondam home of Schiller and Hegel, confiding that he and an audience of highly educated students wondered how they were expected to respond to a brace of perambulating Western Canada bards belting out a guttural, incomprehensible, broken-syllable pseudo-Indian chant – *Nuk! Nuk! Taka! Taka!* – touted as the cutting edge of the nation's poetry. Not even Hölderlin in the throes of terminal dementia ever plunged to such incoherent depths.

The species of ethnological cachet I have bulleted might also explain why, for example, Dionne Brand, who produces by the gross such lines as 'Murdoch and Thompson [*sic*] / owning all the newspapers in the world / is a violation of free speech' – lines which I am bound to say are nothing less than a violation of poetic speech – should be touted as

Canada's Toni Morrison (although the comparison may be more damaging than many suspect). Or why the *International Herald Tribune* should devote a column to the passing of Al Purdy as if he were a figure of any real significance. Or why the poetry and prose of Anne Michaels – the former, it is true, consolingly readable if wholly undistinguished and the latter trading on a borrowed, peregrine glamour – should travel any further than Kenora. Or why L=A=N=G=U=A=G=E feministika Erin Mouré, whose work nobody understands, not even the poet herself to judge from some of her own contextualizing remarks, should be collected in a prestigious international anthology. Or, to stick with fiction for a moment, why a one-note Celtic threnody steeped in banal and portentous sentiment – a very great mischief indeed – can win the IMPAC Dublin Literary Award. A judicious medley of simple sentences and serial clichés strung out over a collection of vignettes makes for an unbeatable combination apparently, especially if it signifies the colonial reverie of the clan.[1] Or why *The English Patient*, *The Blind Assassin* and *Life of Pi*, among the most boring, uninflected and monochromatic novels ever written and published in this country, would somehow meet with mondial applause.[2]

Canlit may be hot these days – I have recently read that it is now enjoying its 'golden age' – but to a sceptical minority it has begun to seem disturbingly frivolous and self-indulgent. I will maintain that Canada enjoys a handful of superb writers but that very few of these have received much attention either abroad or at home. I will argue that we have failed to make the necessary distinction between merit and celebrity on which a vital literary culture is predicated, and I will not scruple to attack those whom I consider mediocre and derivative despite their marquee names, canonical status and commercial success. I will do my utmost to oppose the hasty and unearned sense of accomplishment that our writers and editors seem to take as a given. (E.g., Aritha van Herk *et al.* have recently regaled us with *Due West: 30 Great Stories from Alberta, Saskatchewan and Manitoba.* Great? All thirty? Would not the epithet be a trifle premature?) Otherwise, in failing to speak our minds directly, we begin to resemble those dandiacal and euphemistic wine tasters who manage to find '*petites fleurs blanches*' on the nose of certain wines when nothing recommends the product and there is nothing complimentary to say. Of course, if they believe the little white flowers are really there, we have a far greater problem on our hands.

Irrespective, then, of the praise that has been heaped upon many of these writers beyond our borders and the callow reverence in which they are held at home, I believe they must now be radically unbuttoned (or in relatively good German, un*Knopf*ed). The alternative is to allow things to motor along pretty much as they have since the late fifties / early sixties as critics and reviewers assay their chosen writers with an exaggerated concern amounting at times to a kind of beatification while these latter continue to churn out uniprose novels and trademark McPoetry with complete impunity.

With regard to the latter, there is another possibility we might have to consider, which is that most of the poetry being written in this country is not only distressingly feeble but fundamentally useless, or at any rate *wholly unnecessary*. It is no accident that it takes a private investigator to detect anything of value in the bulk of our poetry, as illustrated by one Wendy Morton, a Vancouver Island–based P. I. who in an article in the Montreal *Gazette* for August 6, 2001, claims among other things that Atwood and Ondaatje are raising the profile of the art. (A practitioner herself, Morton believes poetry is nourishing; of her own poems, she affirms in brave indifference to literary indigestion that 'Anyone who reads them can eat them for lunch.') Be that as it may, apart from maybe a miller's dozen of poets who write responsibly and well and another five or six who show early promise, a moratorium on the publishing of verse would leave no demonstrable vacuum in the land. No one would suffer save for the ostensible victims of an imposed silence who write chiefly for one another while cashing in on institutional largesse. These are poets who have absolutely nothing of any importance to say and who continue to say it interminably. Give them a generous one-time kill fee on the understanding that they would cease publication altogether and the air would clear remarkably.

This is perhaps the place for a short statement of general principles on which I will base my argument in the ensuing. It seems to me that some sort of formal component is obligatory if a poem is not to degenerate into a mere rhapsody of impressions or ultralite reflections. The poet's perceptions need to be *structured* in cadence, metaphor and overall design. For a good poem is always carefully worked and shares the quality of architecture in that it is a construction designed for use, ideally participating in our everyday experience and providing a context for it, as one of the rooms or spaces we live in.[3] The poet's aperçus should also be *grounded* in vivid and memorable language. Finally, the poet should obviously have something of a certain weight to tell us, something which makes a difference, however small, in our scale of values or to our sense of the world and our daily life in it; in other words, a poem must have *substance*, whether that is recognized as new and unprecedented or as a reaffirmation of a material truth we once knew but have perhaps forgotten, dismissed or neglected.

What is absent in so much of our poetry is precisely the structure, ground and substance which are indispensable to the craft and which can only come with patience and slow deliberation. This is why the stanchless prolixity of our current 'makers' and the voodoo principle of effortless self-election they affect are counter-productive. A poem a day keeps the reader away. The truth is, when one contemplates it soberly, that there isn't really very much of consuming interest to write about in the life or from the standpoint of any single, limited individual who wishes to comment on or illumine primary experience unless that person is in some way undeniably exceptional. (Oliver Sachs, say.) The pitiless barrage of poem poem poem / book book book to which we are subjected suggests that our poets suffer collectively from a case of tertiary hubris which augurs poorly for the health of our literature. Who could have imagined there were so many fascinating epiphanies waiting to be recorded and so many sensitive scribes available to record them? In fact, a poem is something that the poet who is writing it should probably approach not only with eagerness and delight but also with trepidation and even with reluctance, and only when the poet honestly feels that the aesthetic experience he or she is shaping has attestable value *for others* (and others who are not necessarily poets themselves), demanding objectification as both artefact and insight. Restraint is a sign of both self-knowledge and charity.

But the dilemma in which we now find ourselves is that the overwhelming majority of our poets – not all but most – have by and large allowed their practice to get away from them. And in their regrettable want of humility and self-interrogation – as those who, to apply a little Browning, 'Participate in Sludgehood / ... banish doubt, / And reticence and modesty alike' – they have tended with a troubling logorrhoeic brashness to produce an ephemeral poetry minus structure, ground and substance. In other words, lacking the complex density of effects and tensile strengths that define the *techné* of the vocation, it is a poetry incapable of 'summoning the dragon' and bearing the enormous pressure of scrutiny per square syllable that poetry inevitably attracts from committed readers over time.[4] I strongly doubt that what Mary Kinzie has favourably called 'the lyric of deprivation' and the 'reduced scale of address' in contemporary poetry can justify 'the retreat from both formal and allusive complexity' that she commends. Dull language remains dull language and a drab, meiotic, recessive poem is still uninteresting despite the premised subtlety for which it is praised and vetted.

As poet Ellery Akers writes, 'I ... practice anger as if it were Italian' ('What I Do'). I realize my intention of defrocking nakedness and the mode in which I pursue it may lead to the standard critical mantra of 'biliousness' and 'negativity' or to charges of self-righteousness, presumption and pontifical imperiousness of temper, as if I regarded myself as the autocrat of the writing table or as someone appointed by the Lord to fulminate and decry. Or even worse, as a somewhat weathered edition of Eminem rapping on about being embarrassed that people still listen to Elvis, 'till someone comes along on a mission and shouts *BITCH*'. Here is a writer, it might be said, with an errant talent for jeremiad. And for all I know, there may be some truth to such an impeachment for no one can escape the penumbra of one's unconscious. This being said, I wish to assure my reader that on the level of conscious intent I have written as I have, plying the counter-discourse of antithetical discrimination, in an effort to distinguish reputability from reputation. The real offence is diffidence and complicity, the major default features of a critical address that insists on treating what is really entry-level work with inordinate respect and even admiration. Here one must draw the line. I am reminded in this connection of my francophone barber, who naturally aspirates her initial vowels: 'Would you like me to straighten h'out the h'eyebrows?' she asks after the cut. I am trying to straighten out the highbrows.

---

1. Thomas Raddall famously dispatched three Toronto writers by referring to

them in terms of clouds: nimbus, cirrus and cumulus. While their identities remain somewhat mysterious, I am assuming such is not the case here.

2. Yann Martel's *Life of Pi* is an interesting case in point. Its much bruited plot similarity to Moacyr Scliar's *Max and the Cats* may be troubling for some but the real problem lies in its narrative tumescence. What might have done for a readable novella bloats to a surplus two hundred or so pages of zoological and nautical detail that gets one's skipping-finger itching. Nor is the prose sufficiently skilled to justify such excess. I suspect that very few will have read the book in its entirety. As for Ondaatje and Atwood, their more recent offerings, *Anil's Ghost* and *Oryx and Crake* respectively, move even further into the Realm of the Drear and Dreadful, in the first case cloyingly 'lyrical' and in the second, saplessly cerebral. Praise is predictably unstinted.

3. To dismiss as many commentators do a responsible poetry with its emphasis on structure, language and substance as irrelevantly or reductively *formalist* is merely an evasion of the demands the craft makes upon its practitioners. Timothy Steele's objection to the term 'formalist', generally used in a pejorative sense, is apposite: 'It suggests, among other things, an interest in style rather than substance, whereas I believe that the two are mutually vital in any successful poem.'

4. The wonderful phrase 'summoning the dragon' is navy patois to describe the sounds of hull resistance heard aboard a diving submarine.

# THE COLOUR OF LITERATURE

> To let yourself be transformed into the emblem of some cause, any cause, or demographic category, and to draw your identity and take your marching orders from it is to kick away your freedom, your independence and your individuality. It is to suspend all these and basically to lose your influence over events that matter to you. You will find that you have forgotten how to speak out views that do not conform to those of the group or that you have been led not to trust such views. You will see life through a very narrow lens and be very much in the control of those who do the defining of the group interest.
>
> – Meg Greenfield, *Newsweek*

I HAVE LONG BEEN uncomfortable with the set of prescriptive beliefs and presuppositions current in the literary and academic communities about the proper way of reading (and writing) literary texts and of aligning their relation with the social world. According to this rationale, if a work of art offends the values or the sensibilities of a particular 'interest group', it may legitimately be sanitized or even suppressed. And when strong ethical pretensions accompany the staking out of potentially dubious rhetorical positions, the predicament is only compounded. A restrictive and dogmatic state of mind begins to pass itself off as an advanced mode of social reasoning, illumining the dark corners of a putatively illiberal (or what amounts to the same thing, overly liberal) and chauvinistic culture. But what we are getting is really censorship in another guise – censorship rendered justifiable and even laudable, *censorship as a form of enlightened thought* though it may be nothing less than the canniest form of intolerance. As philosopher John A. MacKinnon has written, in a letter to the *National Post* for May 21, 2002, 'these days … the blinkered pieties are served up neither by starchy Presbyterians nor self-abnegating Catholics, but by a managerial class that speaks in the voice' of our cultivated, self-appointed public guardians. What we are observing, I suspect, is merely the latest update of Plato's arch-conservative project in *The Republic* and *The Laws*. In merely substituting one target for another, the intellectual vanguard of our society remains as much of an intolerant *arrière-garde* today as it has often been in the past.

I am referring in particular to that burgeoning cohort of neo-neo-colonialists who insist on examining literature, to cite Robert Alter from *The Pleasures of Reading in an Ideological Age*, 'as a symptom of something else [which] requires neither a special liking for literature nor an ability to discriminate between derivative and original, second-rate and first-rate writers'. It becomes especially disconcerting when writers who have acquired a measure of acclaim and are therefore in a position to wield considerable influence take the easy road of received opinion toward approved and indeed trendy destinations. It was thus with some dismay that I read George Elliott Clarke's tendentious article in the *National Post* for Friday May 10, entitled 'Can only white authors teach anti-racism?' – the same letter to which Professor MacKinnon responded above. The assumptions Clarke so readily mobilizes – that literature is colour-specific (witness his use of terms like 'black-authored' and 'white-authored' texts), that novels are primarily sociopolitical documents, that heritage may be conceived as generating literary authenticity and that in the assessment of literary works social questions must take precedence over the fundamental morality of the imagination – have become so prevalent as to be virtually unassailable.

The problem is that beneath the arguments made by Clarke and others like him lurks an ideological motive which both simplifies and distorts the issues they address. We all know that society seethes with innumerable forms of prejudice and that the history of oppression must be grasped and dealt with if we are ever to live in an approximately just world. But in our eagerness to acquire understanding and rectify the ills which bedevil us, we tend to draw distinctions and initiate social movements that are sometimes callow and unreflected and that may very quickly grow fashionable. As a consequence of such haste and superficiality, paradoxes become cripplingly inevitable. In this country, for example, the next step would be to abolish the Charter of Rights and Freedoms since it was 'authored' mainly by a tyrannical constituency of privileged white males who cannot pretend to speak for the disenfranchised and marginal. At the same time, the uncompromising positions so heedlessly adopted by our pseudo-progressives may lead to what may appear as a type of hypocrisy or self-interest. Clarke manifestly had no objection to accepting the prestigious Governor General's Award in an entirely 'white-juried' competition. (Or was this merely a form of author-approved compensation for systemic racial injustice?) And in fact, for many blacks as well as fellow travellers, punishing whites for their indubitable sins has grown into a rather lucrative business – prizes, university posts, high platforms of address – which exploits precisely that pervasive white guilt it affects to denounce.

The great historian Jakob Burckhardt warned us against the intellectual manoeuvres of *les terribles simplificateurs* and he was never more right than at the present moment. Clarke is a case in point. The thesis he develops with respect to the primacy of racial origins over questions of literary merit is distressingly 'black and white' and consorts all too conveniently with the programs of that caste of 'leftish' academics, political cruisers and pop sociologists (and their multitudes of hangers-on) that gather under the general rubrics of Political Correctness and Affirmative Action – a composite, bottom-feeder belief-system that Martin Amis has felicitously called 'the lowest common denomination' and University of Toronto professor John Furedy has dubbed 'velvet totalitarianism'. PC and AfAc represent campaigns which in their *wholesale and undifferentiated* pursuit have served, I'm afraid, to complicate rather than remedy the quandary we are in.

Thus we are confronted with the spectacle of supposedly intelligent people vehemently opposed to what they call 'voice appropriation', condemning writers who presume to write in the voice, idiom or diction of suffering minorities whom their own ancestors helped to oppress. So much for Melville's Queequeg. We find ourselves debating with 'educators' who wish to despoil the curriculum of books, often great books, in which what they target as 'negative stereotypes' and offensive language tend to figure. So much for *Huckleberry Finn*. We gaze in wonderment at literary organizations protesting against discrimination on the grounds of not only race, religion and gender, but talent as well, since a writer is no more responsible for his or her creative equipment than for colour, inherited creed or sex. So much for quality work. We watch the mayor of Washington fire a city official for using the word 'niggardly'. So much for political discourse. We contemplate with some bemusement the legion of tenured academics who indict the Western literary canon as a conspiracy of Dead White Males. So much for Virgil and Dante. We watch the textbook industry, as Diane Ravitch reports in *The Language Police*, phase out *The Little Engine That Could* to avoid the taint of phal-locracy (even though the little engine happens to be female), repudiate dolphins in order not to discriminate against students who live inland and exterminate owls because they are taboo for Navajo Indians. So much for elementary education.

In his own black/white framework, Clarke is unimpeachable when he claims that the works he objects to – *To Kill a Mockingbird* by Harper Lee, *In the Heat of the Night* by John Ball, and *Underground to Canada* by Barbara Smucker – are more about white guilt than about black history. This may be true. And he is surely correct when he suggests that we might redress the balance by listing the works of authors who write from inside their particular worlds and dilemmas. But this is as far as his deposition should be allowed to go.

I would argue against Clarke that the history of white guilt is at least as important as the history of black oppression and that there is no viable reason why these books should not be considered as an appropriate subject of study. Obviously, they should be supplemented (not supplanted) by the works of the specifically implicated – but there is a sense in which we are all implicated. It is a mistake to regard what should be an implicit collaboration as an outright contest. I would argue too that there is a peculiar bias or – let's use the word – prejudice in Clarke's foregrounding of 'black' texts against their apparent lexical competitors. He proposes augmenting the discussion of racism with the 'often superior' works of black authors like Ralph Ellison and Richard Wright. No objection here. But let us be candid about this. We discover names in his catalogue of superiority like Dionne Brand and M. NorbeSe Philip who, in any fair estimation, cannot be assumed to rival Harper Lee. Here, for Clarke, it is plainly skin colour that determines artistic credibility and value, not imaginative power or narrative compe-tence. Finally, and in line with the preceding, I would argue against the facile and invidious distinctions borne by those loaded and patently absurd terms, 'white-authored' and 'black-authored' texts, which Clarke so insouciantly deploys. Insight, verbal authority and creative ability carry no pigmentation, and frankly, I wouldn't care if the author of a given book were a polka-dotted hermaphrodite from Planet X if the book were well-written, honest and compelling. That resonating platitude, voice or cultural 'appropriation', is utterly irrelevant here. Would it not have been a shame if the black woman poet Patricia Smith had been prevented by our new colour demagogues from writing in the persona of a white male supremacist, thus depriving us of an insightful poem like 'Skinhead', which accurately reveals the prejudices and self-justifications of the profoundly alien? Or if Norman Dubie, also a perpetrator of double appropriation, had been deterred by the prevailing ethos from giving us the splendid 'The Negress: Her Monologue of Dark and Light'?

Like Clarke, I too derive from a persecuted people, and I too grew up in a small bigoted community riven with intolerance and hatred. But neither I nor my parents ever objected to Shakespeare's cunning Shylock, a fixture on the curriculum, whom we appreciated as a *character* in a play that expressed contemporary attitudes to the 'interloping' Jew. The fact that Shakespeare wasn't Jewish didn't bother us for a moment and, indeed, we could detect a quality of mercy in our noblest writer which complexified poor Shylock and even established a case for him. And I must say that we were equally fascinated by that other highschool standby, Dickens's suave, cruel and fawning old Jew Fagin, one of the most memorable characters in all of English fiction. It never occurred to us to tar Dickens as an anti-Semite or to view his work as causing irreparable harm to 'our people' or displacing our struggle for recognition. After all, there were more than enough Christian villains in his novels to bring the good name of the Church of England into serious doubt, and besides, as a little reading around revealed, Disraeli went some way toward levelling the playing field with his satire of Dickens in his last novel, *Endymion*. True, I wasn't overly delighted with Mr Daubeney, Trollope's caricature of Disraeli, but one could always compensate by reading George Eliot's – no relation to her apparent namesake – *Daniel Deronda* for a more sympathetic (if rather wooden) treatment of the Jew. Reading, contrary to the current *doxa*, is not a political act, and imaginative writing *as writing* seldom is if it wishes to escape didacticism and preachiness, the kiss of literary death. That is why *Uncle Tom's Cabin* is not a good novel even it was an influential one and also explains why novels (or poems or plays) with a dogmatic component may still survive if story, character and language overwhelm the author's conscious and particular intent. The writer's tools and the way he or she uses them are far more important than the writer's conscious ideas or the writer's obvious identity. Thus Blake could say that Milton, who wrote best when he wrote of Hell, was of the Devil's party without knowing it.

Should a distinct community of readers and parents strenuously object to any or all of the writers I have mentioned above for political or religious or ideological reasons, what would then be the next move? To ban Shakespeare, Dickens, Trollope, Disraeli, Eliot, Stowe, Milton and Blake? There would be no end to the process of exclusion and proscription once we admit the legitimacy of the principle. I realize that many of my co-religionists as well as colleagues and peers would disagree with this argument. The answer, however, lies not in censorship but, so far as possible, in sound, contextual teaching. The repression of any work that is not a deliberate and incontestible species of 'hate literature' is an evil not only in itself but in that it sets a precedent, figuratively as well as literally, for the burning of libraries.

The issue we are treating has to do with the free and passionate sweep of the creative human mind and not with the blurring of boundaries between social and discursive realms. A novel, a poem or a play, like a painting or a symphony, is not *primarily* an ideological document. Certainly it can be used or misused as such, but it is in essence a work of imagination, which offers to enrich and clarify and even trouble and disturb our experience of the world. *And it should be judged this way.* No *literary* work is 'white-authored' or 'black-authored' or 'Jew-authored' or 'male-authored' or 'woman-authored' except in a secondary and tributary sense. (And no literary work is absence-authored as maintained in certain postmodern quarters.) The criteria of judgement are before anything else aesthetic, substantive and talent-based in nature: is the style resourceful and apt, are the characters believable, is the language clear, opulent, effective or energetic, is the structure functional, is the story absorbing and the subject interesting or pertinent in the larger sense, and is the author up to the task? These are the relevant questions. Anything else is only a kind of special pleading, a newly fashionable cliché or the intrusion of a political agenda belonging in another area of discourse and activity. Equal opportunity is a lofty aim but it applies exclusively to providing access into a profession or a social institution, not to the appraisal of results. It is astonishing how the ostensibly revolutionary may become merely another specification of conventional sentiment, devitalizing and quite beside the point despite its ideological gloss. And currency of ideas by no means guarantees their fundamental seemliness or rectitude.

Clarke and those like him should know this if they wish to survive mere cultism or modishness. In literature as in any of the arts, imagination and talent come before everything else. For in terms of origin, all literary works are author-authored.

# THE FLIGHT FROM CANADA

It should be understood first off that from the standpoint of our literature the flight from Canada is not an act of repudiation but in its own elliptical way an act of fidelity or commitment. The sojourn abroad, the annual excursion, the intellectual diaspora, the preoccupation with a transcontinental language rather than a continental identity – all this must be seen in a 'Canadian context' of a wider significance than is usually ascribed to the term.

In particular, there is a strong feeling among some of our better poets that Canadian verse is on the whole lamentably parochial and insular. 'Canadian content' as a local rallying cry, a political expedience, is a perfectly understandable phenomenon, but in poetry its influence is pretty well pernicious. In a country so young, dispersed and undefined as ours, the search for roots, inevitably, becomes paramount in many fields and disciplines, but not without an element of disingenuousness. What begins to unite us is not so much the search but the recognition that the search is good business. It helps politicians get elected, enables merchants to peddle their wares, provides media and university jobs, and hands over to the poets a ready-made subject on which to exercise their indefeasible narcissism in a pretence of disinterestedness and love.

Thus we devote ourselves to the study and rehabilitation of the native peoples, discharging our romantic sensibilities in hymns, elegies and narratives, forms of pastoral nostalgia that, I suspect, are really meant to testify to the aching sensibilities of the poets themselves. We regret the disappearance of the Beothuk and seek to establish a primordial rapport with the lost and the dispossessed in order to relieve the profound anxiety of homelessness that afflicts the 'Canadian' imagination. We absorb the diaries of English ladies beating about the bush and feel gloriously authenticated by such immigrant safaris. We breathe the vestigial dust of the prairies and consider that by virtue of a kind of bio-mental osmosis we have managed to assimilate particles of consciousness that relate

us to our autochthonous predecessors. (See John Newlove's 'The Pride.')
For it is ultimately a quest for ancestors that drives and obsesses us.
The trouble is that it is too deliberate, too self-conscious and artificial,
and culminates in a false sense of identity – as if the aboriginal whose
dust we gallop over with such quickened imaginations will ever
acknowledge us *his* heirs and descendants. We conveniently forget that
the poetic bloodline we seek to consolidate is laced with the blood of
others.

What too many 'Canadian' writers have failed to realize is that the
EskiMohawk and his legends are as foreign to us as Agamemnon and the
House of Atreus. We can never hope to capture, as one well-known poet
assures us we can, 'the ritualistic work of the Canadian native on his
own ground', as if in this way we could magically connect to 'the body's
intelligence.' Forgive me: what rot! There is no continuity of tradition
here, merely a superimposition. And the poet who writes as if he or she
were the conscience of the conqueror, the immaculate witness, the dis-
tressed apologist, the maker of amends, is proficient in nothing so much
as in the art of self-deception. This is not the practice of poetry but the
practice of condescension, an easy Establishment gesture. ('Reworking
Huron or Haida legends into fragmentary poetic narratives,' says Robert
Allen, 'is ... a reactionary scam.') And if one really wants to get
autochthonous about this, one can apply an Algonkin expression and
say that in the sameness of their thinking and writing, these poets are
*nind owiawina*: 'each is another myself,' as any one of these poets can
posit of any other.

Another manifestation of the 'Canadian content' syndrome is that
curious amalgam of nature-and-sociological description that infests
our poetic territory. I should confess at the outset that I don't consider
the descriptive mode as essentially poetic, unless it is elevated to the
plane of metaphor and symbol – and even then it remains problematic.
Perhaps Eliot was not so far wrong when he wrote in *After Strange Gods*
that landscape appeals to the kind of author 'who is interested not at all
in men's minds, but only in their emotions.' Perceptive and compassion-
ate renderings of life in the loneliness surrounding the grain elevator, or
reverent and meticulous descriptions of the Rockies, or anguished
accounts of winter, or recordings of one's feelings in the face of natural
grandeur or desolation have little or nothing to do with poetry, so far as

I can see, for they attribute to landscape a latent adequacy and power while leaving it largely untransformed by imaginative insight. (I have found nothing in our poetry, for example, to compare with Robert Graves' 'Rocky Acres' in which landscape and mind are so tectonically fused as to leave no fault line between them.) As Bruce Taylor instructs us in a poem entitled 'Social Studies',

> The country I live in is a patch of thorns
> below a culvert in a sunken plot
> where burly geese with necks like flugelhorns
> intimidate the pigeons and are shot
> by a district sales manager named Russ.

In poetry the merely factual is merely factitious; the inventory of feeling, whether dry and laconic or passionate and exuberant, is just canonization of self, the exaltation of Russ. The garrigue remains unirrigated.

With these conditions and circumstances in mind, the centrifugal urgency that a small number of our poets have felt may be easily accounted for. If the stereotype 'Canadian' is anything, he is a largely undifferentiated creature, historically in transit, stridently infatuated with the idea of landscape per se, busy assembling a ramshackle identity from mute, refractory materials, and turning his apparent humility before place and time into a subtle form of self-idolatry. As for the poets themselves, they seem on the whole content with inflated reputations at home and, in most cases, massive obscurity abroad. In any event, far too many of our poets have found a *home* in lack of distinctive style coupled with low thematic prime, in the sense that Frost gives the term 'home' in 'The Death of the Hired Man' as 'Something you somehow haven't to deserve.' Which is why poetry can never be a home to the poet, only an itinerary, a perpetual aesthetic trajectory, a constant proving.

The thesis I would stress is that it is precisely the comfortless absence of a secure identity, the rootlessness, the sense of radical alienation which is our greatest gift and blessing. 'A wind not a root is the land's best lover,' chants Brent MacLaine in a very fine poem. Routes, not roots, confer authority upon us. If the poet in this country has one major imperative it is not to write primarily about 'Canadian' themes, to describe the indigenous, but simply to write well about anything and everything in what I have elsewhere called seraphic speech, in language that is charged with vitality and metamorphic power. It is to break down the boundaries of our insularity, to take all place and time as our patrimony with a sort of Verulamian relish and ambition. Rosanna Leprohon, writing in the Preface to her 1864 novel *Antoinette de Mirecourt*, held it as an article of faith that 'Although the treasures of 'the old world' are ever open to us, and our American neighbours should continue to inundate the country with reading-matter ... yet Canadians should not be discouraged from endeavouring to form and foster a literature of their own'. The sentiment is just, but I would extend her argument by claiming that, in order to 'form and foster a literature of [our] own,' we need most at this point in our development to avoid the forcing-ground mentality that has come upon us and to recognize that we are most our own when, to adapt Bacon's apothegm, we feel free to take all knowledge for our province, not our province for all knowledge. This caveat should not prevent us, of course, from treating of our province, but should serve to remind us that our province is only one small part of a universe that beckons gloriously, and that language is the light in it.

Canada, after all, is not Zion. If we have a country its psychic equivalent is difference and otherness, the feeling for unexplored horizons, and, really, as *poets*, as lovers of language, as privileged transgressors of the commonplace, we have more in common with ground-breaking figures like Blake and Spenser than with conservative placeholders like Carman and Sangster. Nor should we be misled by the supposed innovations of an Arthur Stringer or a W. W. E. Ross who, located conventionally at the origins of the modern movement in Canada, were not poets at all but arid and predictable journeymen versifiers.

All this as I have said is not to place an embargo on 'Canadian' writing, but rather to try and stay clear of centripetal passions and the kind of mediated jingoism that doubles for inspiration – the Ernie-at-the-wheel-of-the-van-driving-through-Saskatchewan syndrome, to cite from a poem of Dale Zieroth – and to revel instead in our freedom to travel extensively in all the realms of language, thought, feeling, time and place. And naturally to carry with us adequate provisions to victual the journey, most notably imagination and wit, like Moll Flanders' hamper of brandy and lemons to circumvent debility as well as insipidness, the scurvy of our calling. There is, obviously, nothing to hinder us from returning again and again, but it should be emphasized that one cannot truly settle in Canada, especially if one happens to be a writer, unless one has spent considerable time elsewhere, and continues to get out from time to time, hopefully in reality and certainly in imagination. And as *writers* our passport to *authentic* selfhood resides far more in language and technique than in the fetish of content, provided our themes are life-related. I am not speaking here of the spurious cosmopolitanism that A. J. M. Smith set up against a presumed native tradition but, as I have suggested, of nothing more but manifestly nothing less than the ability to write good lines in appropriate forms about important subjects. The source and criterion for poetic calibre are talent, discipline, a certain seriousness of mind and a passion for language held together in a single amalgam of sustained purpose and creative delight.

As for that desideratum called identity, it is not to be constructed by intent nor can a national reality be conjured by decree or subsidy. When such becomes the case it leads inescapably to gasconade in politics, messianism in religion, and in literature to a quaint pretentiousness or a sterile ostentation. The insistent focus on the particular does not necessarily ensue in the resonantly universal, but as often as not in an encysted narrowness that writers such as Flaubert and Yeats relentlessly condemned. Unless one is blessed with genius and judgement, numbering the streaks of the tulips (in Dr Johnson's phrase from *Rasselas*) may lead not to concrete presence but chromatic myopia. I readily grant that the universality we seek as poets may require a speech 'rooted' in the colloquial, but it also needs a sense of diction and form that links us to the whole tradition of verse, certainly of English-language verse, from auroral times to the present. It may require a feeling for place, a lively and intimate appreciation of landscape 'not yet written on by history' (in the words of Frank Scott from 'Laurentian Shield') but must also be qualified and enhanced by the recognition of landscape as intrinsically symbolic or as an embodiment of spirit, that is, as something that must be effectively deliteralized. No less crucially, it demands an independence of mind willing to chart its own course and stake out its own territory in defiance of the schools and the buzzwords of the day, *wherever that imperative may take it.* We

29

might well take as our motto an epigram from Henri Coulette, entitled 'Overture':

Stand back and give me room.
Cogito ergo zoom.

Canadian poets have been given the unique opportunity of making an equally unique identity for themselves as a function of their *unbehaust* condition, hewing the wilderness of self into an unprecedented order. In so doing, identity is solidly founded in difference, in the fact that each poet can work up the materials of place and language into that signature alloy we call individual style. The saving paradox is that the Canadian poet is *ideally* Canadian only inasmuch as he or she is distinctively unlike any other Canadian poet. Merely compare two of our finest, Charles Bruce and Irving Layton, to see the territory we can chart into the special character of a national poetry that revels in disparity and idiosyncrasy, in deviation from a preconcerted norm. Living where we do, we are permitted to become variations on a theme; indeed, the variation *is* the theme.

Sir John A. Macdonald once said that Canada has 'too much geography and too little history'. The geography remains, the history will come, but meanwhile Canada has too little individual self and too much artificial unity. Our poets are most truly Canadian not when they are 'Canadian' but when they are eclectic, seeking tributaries from everywhere to swell the national brook. They are most truly faithful when they are most impenitently promiscuous. The Canadian exigency is, finally, synthesis. As Susan Glickman points out in her excellent *The Picturesque and the Sublime: A Poetics of the Canadian Landscape*, with specific reference to Thomas Cary's *Abram's Plains* (1789), the poet manages to reconcile and conflate a dual imperative that includes 'both the pastoral "Zephyrus" and the invigorating "northern gale"', that is, the traditional and the local, endorsing the continuity between two worlds and a double source of inspiration. Eventually the synthesis will 'take' and an identity will gradually arrive, a rich and composite identity, hybrid and syncretic, yet no less genuine for all that. But we must absolutely drop this 'Canadian' shibboleth that so restricts and oppresses, this puerile, involuted and autistic pursuit of our *mythical* selfhood, and cultivate instead a healthy indifference to that collective self-consciousness which is at present one of our most distinguishing, if least distinguished, characteristics.

# ACORN, LEMM
# AND OJIBWAY

A RECOLLECTION OF MILTON ACORN

Ask me: Does his ghost walk?
How could you spot it in a particular place
When his ghost is everywhere?

– 'Tom Thomson's Photo'

I FIRST MET MILTON ACORN in the early sixties when I was a fresh-
man at McGill, just arrived in Montreal from a small town in the Lau-
rentians and beginning to discover that there were poets in the world
besides the three Williams and a few others who colonized the high
school curriculum. There were even *Canadian* poets, I learned, apart
from John McCrae.

One of these was Milton Acorn who made up for his absence from
anthology and reading circuit by running a small coffee house, called
The Place, in the student ghetto with Bryan McCarthy, now starting to
make his reputation, and Joe Sage, a grizzled veteran of life's wars.
It consisted of one claustrophobic ground-floor room filled with
smoke, wannabe poets, the smell of mimeograph fluid and chipped
cups of devastatingly bad coffee. Living quarters were upstairs. Sage
seemed to be the organizing figure with McCarthy gliding about from
table to table like a mystical compère and Acorn providing the *son
et lumière*. The Place hung on for maybe a year or even a little longer.
Eventually, Acorn left for more propitious climes. Joe Sage disappeared
never to be seen again. And Bryan McCarthy palavered his way to local
celebrity for *Smoking the City* and the central table at the Café Bistro on
Mountain Street, then simply faded out like a plume of marijuana
smoke, or, for that matter, like most Montreal poets in the anarchic
sixties.

But it is Milton Acorn I remember most vividly, giving his nightly oracular recitations, stomping up and down the among the tables bellowing poems like *I Shout Love* in a voice that can only be described as megaphonic. On one unforgettable night, and for no apparent reason, as I sat shyly and inconspicuously in the smokiest corner, Acorn – as burly a poet as they came – suddenly grabbed me by the arm, dragged me upstairs to his shambles of a room, and flung me on the bed where I cringed in a paroxysm of terror. Then he took a sheaf of poems from his worktable and without any preamble began to read them aloud, pacing back and forth, pausing only to light a cigar. This went on for about half an hour. I was sixteen years old, still very much a rustic who thought a cappuccino was 'a cup of Chino' and that poems were curious verbal artefacts written mainly by dead people. Milton Acorn scared the bejesus out of me but when I had realized I wasn't about to be raped or murdered, I was able to concentrate somewhat on the poetry, which I found at the time entirely incomprehensible. Eventually he let me go but not before I had experienced my first initiation into the raw problematics of the Muse, understanding nothing yet stunned to attention.

It didn't seem to matter whether or not I knew what was going on or could assimilate the poetry. He had the *presence*. Why he selected me on that evening as his victim and beneficiary I have never managed to figure out. Maybe he recognized a fellow hick who needed a bit of shaking up. As the years added up to our mutual cost we would meet every now and then at readings and suchlike events and always got on cordially, though I suspect that Milton had forgotten completely what had been for me a momentous rite of passage but for him merely one more in a multitude of turbulent encounters. Still, in some profound sense, Milton Acorn was my first poetic mentor, the first poet who introduced me to the Ojibway of the craft.

Five or six years ago I had a very strange dream involving my unwitting benefactor, which obviously harks back to that weird episode. We were sharing a room in a decrepit tenement in some nameless, grey, perpetually rainy city. Milton was asleep on the bottom bunk while I lay awake in the narrow cot above, staring at the ceiling. Suddenly I became aware that the rain had begun to seep into the room and that the water level was rising alarmingly. At that moment someone knocked at the door and announced that there was a telephone call for me. 'Who is it?' I asked. The anonymous tenant replied, 'It's Margaret Chatwood.' 'Oh,' I said, 'then I'd better get it.' I sloshed through knee-deep water into the hall to where the small, black, old-fashioned telephone lay on an oval night table, picked up the receiver and said hello. Silence. Hello again. Silence. It seemed like I waited an unconscionable time but could not elicit a single word from the non-chatty presence on the other end. Meanwhile the water continued to rise. Finally I decided this was going nowhere and hung up the receiver. I returned to the room where Milton was still asleep, climbed up to my bunk and proceeded to study the ceiling again, fascinated by the patterns in the wooden laths and joists. Soon the water was lapping at my ears and nostrils. 'Milton,' I cried, 'if we don't get out we're going to drown,' and at that moment I woke up.

I have no idea what the dream was all about although the wood motif is obvious – Chatwood, Acorn, the fact that Milton was a carpenter, the wooden ceiling – and the obvious irony that Chatwood had absolutely nothing to say (which I believe is the case anyway, for Atwood is the kind of poet whose lack of substance and variety has never interfered with prolixity, that is, the kind of poet whom Acorn abominated). Clearly I had identified with my dreammate in an important way and intuited that we were both in danger of going under in some sort of bleak, primeval and confined environment. Canada? Or did I unconsciously recall those wonderful lines from his *On Speaking Ojibway* which had somehow trickled into the dream but with an ominous change in implication?

> Best speak in the woods beside a lake
> getting in time with the watersounds.
> Let vibrations of waves sing right through you
> and always be alert for the next word
> which will be yours but also the water's.

Or, since there is no arrogance in dreams, did I imagine we were like Dante, whom we both loved (though Acorn claimed in the title to a curious sonnet that he was 'in hot pursuit of Chaucer'), exiles lost in a dark mysterious wood and – in an access of wished-for affinity with a greatness we would never in the real world be able to approximate – *mi ritrovai per una selva oscura*? But, oddly enough, the anxiety I experienced in the dream was chiefly (and perhaps vicariously) for Milton, who refused to awaken to the threat of oblivion.

It is for this reason that when I chanced upon Richard Lemm's fine biography, *Milton Acorn: In Love and Anger* (a worthy successor to Chris Gudgeon's *Out of This World: The Natural History of Milton Acorn*), I seized upon it and read it through in one sitting more or less the way Acorn inexplicably seized upon the terrified student and did not release him until he had finished *his* reading. For such a book was long overdue about this craggy and inescapable figure, this voice crying in the Canadian wilderness – a voice whose claims, rants, visionary accents, raucous timbre (that did not hide a certain elegiac plangency), patriarchal force and direct proletarian mode of address had been far too often neglected and at times even derided. It is true that Milton Acorn wrote a hit-and-miss kind of poetry: when he was off, he was embarrassing, but when he was on, the rightness of diction, phrase, line and cadence – the words following the contour of his speaking voice – and the importance of his subject revealed a master in his element. And this is what comes through in Lemm's painstaking and affectionate biography.

Lemm does exemplary justice (not just ice, as critical biographers are sometimes wont to do – see, for example, Elspeth Cameron's hatchet job on Irving Layton) to his subject, offering in the first half or so of the book a detailed account of the poet's wanderings in the mazy urban thoroughfares of the Mainland cities, his various encounters with people whom he either mesmerized or alienated (Acorn, of course, was the arch-polarizer), his troubled relations with the official literary community in this country, and his unfortunate Shrek-like marriage to the ineffable and deceptively fionine Gwendolyn MacEwen. What Lemm gives us in effect is the chronicle of a poet who always seemed to be leaving, usually prematurely. But it is in the second part of the book that Lemm, liberated from the necessary but occasionally clogging minutiae every biographer has to domesticate in order to establish a professional context for his purposes, wings toward an extended peroration on Acorn's achievement and his renewed nuptials with the Island he had abandoned so many times, thus turning a faithful chronicle into a rich celebration of the *nostos* of the latter years.

Here the prose style, unfailingly competent, really begins to soar as Lemm warms to his theme and sympathetically observes the poet in his natural environment. He shows him moving among family, friends and neighbours and setting about consolidating his powerful, anti-colonial, Minago voice, the anger it could express so vigorously always tempered by love, in a series of poems that are now becoming a part of *our* landscape. 'The figure in the landscape [that makes] the land-scape,' as the celebrated poem has it, is very much Milton Acorn:

> His beard may be like a sprucetree upside down
> Or scraggy from recent Indian mixture;
> But whatever his eyecolour was a moment before;
> Preoccupied with work, keen with observation,
> Wild in a laugh or soft and genial …

As if knowing that the figure who to some very real extent made our landscape (at least in part) is in danger of disappearing in it, Lemm gets love and anger into his deposition too – muted anger at the disregard the poet intermittently suffered until it was nearly too late but evident love for a generous spirit who spoke for the forgotten and the oppressed, for those who were also disregarded. The book works, finally, not so much as chronicle but as a kind of *summoning*, a bringing back to our regard of a poet who, as so often in the past, left before his time had come. Owing partly to Lemm's passion and eloquence and partly to Acorn's own increasingly vivid, revenant presence in these pages – perhaps the same weird emanation of authoritative selfhood on which I remarked earlier – we begin uncannily to feel, as we proceed toward the twin conclusions of the book and the life, as though we were inhabiting Acorn's own major poem, a sort of displaced confession entitled *The Natural History of Elephants*, where 'Death is accorded no belief and old friends / are constantly expected.'

Thanks to efforts like Lemm's, we may still enjoy the company of a poet who became the virtuoso of departures but who was never properly appreciated for what he left behind: a bardic voice that contin-ues to resound with the authentic tones of a possible country that may one day, however unlikely it may seem, come into veridical existence, a country whose first language will be Ojibway, which Acorn defines as

Words always steeped in memory
and hope that makes sure
by action that it's more than hope,
That's Ojibway, which you can speak in any language.

# THE TROUBLE WITH ANNIE

It is time the stone made an effort to flower,
time unrest had a beating heart.
    – Paul Celan, 'Corona'

'Don't blow smoke on my cricket!' (Stuart McLean)
'It's already dead.' (Peter Gzowski)
    – *Morningside*

I HAVE LONG SUSPECTED that the genus of drab, inertial poetry that now permeates the literary scene may be put down not only to the poet's ambition to write abundantly whatever the consequences but, generally speaking, to the desire to acquire status in an official community of impresarios, critical strategists and bravura players. Of course the job cannot be done by the poet alone but requires the complicity of an audience willing to accept inferior work and a cartel of influential critics eager to encourage it. Evidence for this claim is not hard to find. Anne Carson's sudden cometary prominence provides us with a textbook example of how the mediocrity industry works in our time, attuned not to merit or talent but to celebrity – 'A celebrity,' said Daniel Boorstin, 'is someone who is famous for being famous' – , bestowing the power of incumbency on substandard writers. It is therefore largely oblivious to quality, content, genuine facility with language, and moral and aesthetic grist. Look closely at Carson's practice, without preconceptions if possible, and you will find a surprising lack of grapple there, a frivolity and affectation that should rightfully call the work and the thinking that presumably innervates it into question.

Sometimes, of course, the poetry appears to be 'original' when it is only eccentric, mannered or even freakish, as an attentive reading should immediately make clear. How, then, does Carson get away with it? How is it that such material has not been immediately interpellated and exposed? Is it because readers will often tend to question their own intelligence rather than the poet's competence when confronted by the capricious, the prosaic, the nebulous or the superficial? But if one scrutinizes these poems dispassionately, one hardly knows where to begin, and once having done so, where to end in disclosing the docetic counterfeit of a production that is all surface and no body. I will confine myself to only a few examples, with the proviso that it be understood that almost any other specimen would do equally well in demonstrating the absence of genuine vision and marrow. Consider a short piece entitled 'That Strength':

That Strength. Mother, dug out. Hammered, chained,
dislocated, weeping, sweeping, tossed with its
groaning, hammered, hammering bolts
off death. Shaken and damning
stars. Unjudgeable. Knife. Un
breakable on grindstones
that strength,
Mother
Broke.

This typical Carson poem with its stringing together of disjointed words and phrases, supposedly purging verbal surfeit in order to reveal truth but reading mainly like the residue of a débridement procedure, does not *in itself* deserve serious inspection. Its pared-down, fragmented, *wounded* style appears to derive in large measure from Paul Celan's habitual practice, founded in his grievous and alienating exposure to the Nazification of his beloved German *Sprache*, a truly demonic encounter of which Carson has no comparable and validating experience. (Even its queer verb-closure seems to resemble the conclusion of Celan's DEW poem: 'the Lord broke the bread/the bread broke the Lord.') Nor can I refrain from posing a few simple, normative questions. What is the *clear* sense of the piece, if indeed there is one? (I maintain that despite the many shades and possibilities of meaning a poem may yield, there should always be a 'clear sense' or *cantus firmus* from which we may take our bearings.) Is there a single line *qua* line (or even a phrase) we might single out as striking or memorable? Does it radiate an impression of lexical authority? Does anything hide beneath the broken

THE TROUBLE WITH ANNIE

glitter of its verbal surface? Do we feel tempted or motivated to make it an organic part of our mental life, committing it to memory if we had the time to do so? Are we *really* impressed or edified by so autistic a consummation? The scholarship for which she is celebrated merely exacerbates her overall performance. For instance, her customary allusions to Greek begetters, such as Mimnermus, Stesichorus and Simonides, and the attempt to link these, especially the latter, by way of proleptic minimalism not only with her own production but with the thought of a German-Jewish poet like Paul Celan who lived through the Shoah, are both anachronistic and jejune. The relation she is tracking in *Economy of the Unlost* between a fifth-century Greek and a twentieth-century Jew seems entirely incommensurable. The 'Nothing' Simonides supposedly privileges – the capitalization of the word is Carson's illegitimate attempt at conceptual reification and is foreign to Greek usage in this context – has 'nothing' in common with the 'Nothing' that Celan experienced in a concentrationary century as the scion of a persecuted people. Thinking of something that is absent is a different form of negation from taking absence into the centre of one's affective life, that is, from becoming it or dying of it. To insist on their equivalence is a hypostatic form of substance abuse.[1]

It remains a moot question which is more precarious, the scholarship or the poetry it often vitiates. As a particularly telling illustration of the former, see her analysis in *Economy* of Celan's puzzling and well-known 'NO MORE SAND ART', which is disturbing in its heavy-handed dependence on John Felstiner's *Paul Celan: Poet, Survivor, Jew* and in her cavalier treatment of the Holocaust, as we will see shortly when we consider the gratuitous levity of her analysis of vowel dissipation in a hypothetical Hebrew translation of the poem in question. As for the few interesting things she does have to say, these are cribbed almost verbatim from Felstiner. Quoting his book in a footnote with respect to only *one item* of resident obscurity in the poem tends to distract the reader from noticing her various borrowings, which looks very much like evading detection by apotropaic citation. Cite your source in one small point – especially if your source is esoteric – and under cover of reputability you can get away with wholesale annexation.

Thus in a very compact space Carson duplicates *all* of Felstiner's main points and references, from Celan's 1948 *Sand from the Urns* to Mallarmé's 'A Throw of the Dice' to the question-and-answer binary of the poem to the rhetorical question 'Your song, what does it know?' Synonyms appear to carry on the work of evasion inaugurated by a citational stratagem: Felstiner's 'reduced', as it seems to me, becomes her 'economy', his 'admit no art' becomes her 'repudiate a kind of art' – and we are not even speaking of the general tenor of the two studies which are pretty well identical. Even her attempt to account for the disintegration of the fused word 'Deepinsnow' to its constituent vowels at the end of NO MORE SAND ART derives from a suggestion of Felstiner's, but takes it further than Felstiner, for reasons of tact, is willing to go. Felstiner (a bit misleadingly) writes: 'But translated into Hebrew, which has no vowel letters, this poem would verge on silence – a testimony to the literal truth that Celan sought.' Whereas Carson clinches the argument in a concluding tag that is deeply troubling: 'For one cannot but think, watching 'Deepinsnow' melt away, that if this poem were translated into Hebrew, a language whose vowels don't appear in some printed texts, it would vanish even before its appointed end. *As did many a Hebrew*' (italics mine). The tactlessness is compounded by an unintentional irony that scuttles the point anyway; it is precisely the vowels (reproducible in Hebrew *pintelech*) that remain at the end of the poem.[2]

Anyone who doubts this overall indictment should examine pages 219–20 of Felstiner's book (Yale University Press, 1995) and compare them with pages 115–16 of Carson's (Princeton University Press, 1999). In a similar vein, Stephen J. Willet twice points out in an article in the *Bryn Mawr Classical Review* (February 2000) that several of Carson's Celan translations in *Economy* are 'word-for-word identical to Michael Hamburger's without any attribution'. Moreover, her study of the poet 'makes no original contribution and is largely recycled Celan scholarship'. As for poor Simonides, Willet regards him as the victim of Carson's 'slapdash' approach resulting in a 'mistranslation'. Interestingly, Roger Kimball in a 1991 TLS review of the classics journal *Arion* had already taken Carson to task for intellectual appropriation and poor scholarship, or in his own words, for 'sycophantizing Aristotle's *Poetics*' and producing 'a piece of literary theorizing *à la mode* that begins with an egregious mistranslation of Aristotle and never really recovers'.

I have focused, perhaps excessively, on the scholarship because Carson constitutes a special case in which the double lack of fibre and talent is more readily ascertainable in the academic work than in the poetry, though it will be found there too. Take, for example, a poem called 'Freud (1rst draft)', one of many such 'drafts' or patently unfinished pieces that clutter her *Men in the Off Hours*. There we discover that

> Freud spent the summer of 1876 in Trieste
> researching hermaphroditism in eels.
>
> In the lab of zoologist Karl Klaus
> he dissected
> more than a thousand to check whether they had testicles.
>
> 'All the eels I have cut open are of the tenderer sex,'
> he reported after the first 400.
> Meanwhile
>
> the 'young goddesses' of Trieste were proving
> unapproachable.
> 'Since
>
> it is not permitted
> to dissect human beings I have
> in fact nothing to do with them,' he confided in a letter.

As it happens, much of the poem's content and even its general phrasing seems poached from Peter Gay's *Freud: A Life for Our Time* (Doubleday, 1989, pages 31, 32) and, along with the quoted passage from Freud's letters (also mentioned by Gay), chopped up, rearranged slightly and fitted into stanzas. Some readers – I am obviously not one of them – may feel that such unattributed borrowings are not wholly illegitimate but the real question is: *where is the poetry?* For these are merely boilerplate verses that we could find in the prose of journalist or biographer *in precisely this syntactical form.*

Time for a reality check. Carson may be our newest pedestalized inamorata but the fact is – and I say this unabashedly – her work appears to be chiefly sleight-of-hand, both the scholarship and the poetry. Although Milton assuredly demanded too much of poets when he affirmed in the *Apology for Smectymnuus* that 'he who would not be frustrate of his hope to write well hereafter in laudable things, ought himself to be a true poem, that is, a composition and pattern of the best and honorablest things,' the asymptotic approach to this ideal remains crucial. As Celan once said, 'only true hands write true poems.' Still, if the work is so obstreperously bad, how account for the reputation? This is mainly spread and consolidated by editors, critics and reviewers whose bookish expertise – regardless of whatever previous accomplishments they may licitly boast – can be described in far too many instances as a kind of higher Sesame Street word-and-number recognition faculty. They tend to sound like sciolistic Counts and half-educated Big Birds, reacting with manic delight to the lexical doits and clippings and allusions that Carson-type poetry provides for their enlightenment. Sometimes I find myself thinking that Carson actually doesn't exist but is rather the creation of a couple of heavyweight critics and a swarm of quailing lightweights straggling along in their wake like a troop of puppets in their solferino suits, all brandishing the same set of clichés about Carson's 'quirky wit' and 'surprising juxtapositions'.

Thus Rachel Barney in a review of Carson's translation of Sophocles' *Electra* for the *National Post* (July 21, 2001) speaks of her poetry as 'rich and startlingly odd' but cannot readily digest the translation itself. Barney tries valiantly to get around this inconvenience by opining that the tone is 'at once powerful and disorientingly banal' and that 'Carson's toying with the register of sitcom must be deliberate.' I doubt it very much: a literary vice cannot be morphed into a translational virtue. This is merely a last-ditch rescue effort, an attempt to avoid the issue by sententious extenuation. The piece sounds like a sitcom for highbrows not only because superior hackwork may be a function of Carson's peculiar talent but because she does not have the poetic apparatus to mediate a strong, demotic original in the first place. In this way, a career is built up by a relentless concatenation of more or less identical platitudes, leading to what Seamus Heaney, taking a page from Chomsky, has called the 'manufactured consensus' to which poetry should properly immunize us. What we are dealing with is only a suburban legend.

The spectacle continues. Harold Bloom, who has already begun to call his credentials into question by his recent bardolatric profusions, is now risking his reputation further by adopting Carson (to accompany the equally gormless John Ashbery) as poetry's last best hope, and Susan Sontag is plunging into critical eclipse with a similar endorsement. Misconceiving opacity as complexity and a farouche coquettishness for unsuspected depths, Guy Davenport compares her to Arnold, Joyce and Dante. Elizabeth Lowry, a tutorial fellow in English at Greyfriars College, Oxford, swoons down six columns of the *London Review of Books*, obviously smitten by 'one of the most seductive writers around' like Carson's own 'lovesick Geryon' thrilling to the voice of Herakles. Don Summerhayes writing in the *Literary Review of Canada* eliotically reminds us that we might have 'to shift the rankings of all the other poets to accommodate this one', yet blithely observes that her texts are full of the kind of thing that 'you do not yet know what it is to formulate' and refers with quixotic wonder to 'whatever it is that Carson does'. Ignorance never stopped an infatuated reviewer. (Summerhayes, a poet, might have remembered a couple of his own lines: 'I have the evidence and can testify, I know it is perfectly ordinary.') Helen Dunmore, chair of the T. S. Eliot Award jury, raves over Carson's 'taut, lyrical, erotic, plain-spoken and highly charged' style although every one of these prattling epithets is emphatically belied by the work itself, except perhaps for 'plain-spoken', the exergue of an otherwise fey esotericism. Fraser Sutherland in the *Globe and Mail* adduces lines 'that would make any other poet murderously envious' and the *New York Times* reviewer trumpets: 'Carson writes in language any poet would kill for.' I had always thought the real test was whether poets write in language they would be willing to die for, but since we are in such a bloodthirsty mood I might ask the reader if he or she would be ready either to kill or to die for the unchallenged right to declaim the following pseudo-Catullan litany: 'Hate hate hate hate hate hate hate hate hate / Hate hate hate hate hate hate love hate'? Or to ask with such ineffable lucidity, 'Can you pause in the thought / that links origin / and tendency?' (Incidentally, can you?) And this is watermark Carsonese.

Back-cover blurbs are especially compromising. 'Amazing,' gushes Alice Munro apropos *Autobiography of Red*. 'I haven't discovered any writing in years that's so marvelously disturbing.' I suppose Munro must be referring to such notable lines (which come by the bale) as 'I better be getting home. / Okay' or 'Somewhere a door slammed. / Leaves tore past the window.' Carson writes a 'glittering prose poetry that is both timely and timeless', says Katherine Govier in – what else? – *Time*, unaware that the oxymoron 'prose poetry' gives the show away completely. Michael Ondaatje considers Carson as 'the most exciting poet writing in English today' – but then Ondaatje has also sponsored the work of bp Nichol and is the author of *The English Patient.* The beat goes on and on.

I confess, then, that there are moments when I cannot help wondering whether there is not some sort of professional scam going on, an aspect of what Laurence J. Peter and Raymond Hull call the Peter Principle. In other words, Carson may be the recipient of the benefits of an upward displacement assigned by critics who cannot surrender the hermeneutical cachet she confers, thus allowing her to profit from a type of pseudo-promotion the purpose of which is to delude those outside the hierarchical structure. As a result, an erratic scholar finds herself the beneficiary of 'percussive sublimation' and is now – a recondite poet! One thing is certain. Our critics and reviewers have invested so heavily in the Carson phenomenon that she has become practically unstoppable, a gigantic pyramid scheme no one can blow the whistle on without the entire edifice tumbling down on their heads.

This need to chase the limousine may explain why reviews are beginning increasingly to sound like extended blurbs, which is particularly true of all the little, nameless, unremembered acts of blindness and of praise, i.e., the myriad sampler articles written by the bit players and small-time brokers who effectively do the bidding of Big Applish windbags or of donnish swains and dowsabells to carry the reputation forward into the field of public consciousness. Like the burghers of Schilda in the old Oberhessen tale, they are busy scooping up the night in buckets. For example, a local reviewer, Michael Springate, is as typically unrestrained in his adulation of the poet as he is embarrassing in the passages he isolates for special commendation, which any sensible reader would realize undercut his intentions. In an appraisal of Carson's farrago of essaylets and poems, *Men in the Off Hours*, which appeared in the Montreal *Gazette* (June 17, 2000), Springate asks us to relish such presumably exquisite lines as

'It smells of burning.'

The mother remains alone.

    The wall is subtly different from hour to hour. Season to season.

        Whitish.

           Scalded.

           Sprayed with dawn.

(followed in the actual poem by several more exemplars of equal dowdiness and culminating in the next section in a direct quote from Lenin, 'The purpose of terrorism is terror'). Or again:

    Akhmatova's son Lev was arrested in 1933 (released), 1935

                                          (released),

        1938 (not released).

    She came to the wall to stand in line.

Et cetera. (The stanza continues: 'Inner prison of the NKVD on Shpalernaya Street. / Then Kresty prison across the Neva.') What Springate does not say or maybe even suspect is that these expository lines seem *conceptually* downloaded from Akhmatova's prose anti-preface to her 'Requiem' on the assumption, apparently, that Akhmatova is not competent to speak for herself. The original passage is certainly moving in its context as a prose reminiscence – 'I spent seventeen months in the prison lines of Leningrad,' the Russian poet writes, and lays out the circumstances that impelled her to describe the experience – but the hubris implicit in Carson's gesture prejudices the reading of verses that are already problematic as poetry. Far better to go to the poetry of Akhmatova herself, the poetry of genuine witness and suffering and the only creditable account of the experience hinted at in the preliminary exposition:

        And not for myself alone I pray,

        but for all who stood with me then,

        in savage frost and in July's blaze,

        beneath that red blinded wall.

(David Ward, writing in *PN Review* 139 on Carson's appropriation of Akhmatova, also comments on the 'evident gulf in emotion and technique from the original to the copy'.)

Like Springate and so many others, Derek Webster, in yet another tributary review that appeared in the same newspaper for March 3, 2001, weightily opines that Carson 'has been changing the face of contemporary literature not unlike the way T. S. Eliot and *The Waste Land* did earlier this [*sic*] century'. She has the effect on readers, apparently, of 'making them wonder if they've ever truly seen anything – self, lover, story, country – anything at all'. Webster does not pause to consider whether enough of the material he praises might not eventually induce a state of forgetfulness or fuzzy-mindedness perilously akin to his own and make readers wonder nostalgically if they have ever truly seen literary artefacts – criticism, poetry – any such things at all, before.

*Ethos anthropo daimon* (character is fate). And perhaps to some extent the Heraclitean dictum also works in reverse. How we respond to a situation is a function of character but character in its making requires a situation, which it either confronts directly or perceives (or disambiguates) imaginatively. It is in that sliding and reversible relation between *ethos* and *daimon*, character and fate, genetics and environment, self and situation that a style is formed that survives its occasion and defines centrally and actively something we may think of as a poetic essence – which we find indisputably in Akhmatova and Celan. But with reference to the style and sensibility I am decorticating in these pages, there is very little we may call original and fervent in itself and certainly not much in the way of a situation, whether historical or metaphysical, to which it *formatively* responds. If, as Mark Doty says, the process of drafting a poem is 'a conversation between what arises and what's willed' – a variation of the *ethos/daimon* nexus – then my point is that in this poetry what arises is negligible and what's willed is only unsponsored self, turning the conversation into a recursive monologue. In comparison with the masterful figures above, Carson's economy of loss is not an economy of scale and the experience she registers justifies neither the evacuated style nor the lowering solemnity, neither the refusal of adornment nor the affectation of lexical reduction. Drabness is not in itself a sign of authenticity and creative indolence does not betoken a lien on poetic rectitude. Despite the valedictory attempt at deep feeling we find in the concluding pages of *Men in the Off Hours*, I suggest that a chunk of didactic prose, a couple of crossouts and an endpiece photograph of mother and daughter sunning on the wharf do not evoke the loss of the *Shekhinah* – the feminine element within the divine – with which Celan associated his mother's death or qualify as a modern 'Requiem' or ESPENBAUM, among the most moving of Celan's poems.

Yet it must be admitted that she is very good at giving the impression of being poised on the cutting edge of her alleged discipline, the *tricoteuse* of intertextual purling. Consider as an illustration of this the elegy for her mother touched on above, entitled 'Appendix to Ordinary Time', where her fashionable play with crossouts in two passages extracted from Virginia Woolf's papers brings up by implication Derrida's ostensibly daring *écriture sous rature* (Derrida is mentioned elsewhere in the book) and puts one in mind of Stephen Potter's elegiac poem, 'Carved', which appeared in the November/December 1999 issue of *The American Poetry Review* (where Carson has previously published). Potter, who also likes to fool around with typography, prints among many similar instances: '~~sunlight, bare orchard, my heart~~ / ~~flew aloof ... this body~~/a persona to carve in stone.' 'Crossouts ... are like death,' Carson informs us in between the two she cites, and 'Death hides right inside every shining sentence.' (Maybe like the 'bronzy glint' of Potter's menacing knife.) Not to leave anything open to question, italics accentuate whatever point is being made among the different font styles, Potter's in the body of the text and Carson's as marginalia: *'such/abandon/ment/such/rapture'*. Such nonsense.

But the act of critical liberation involved in *our* recognizing this species of negative biomimicry will require prodigies of unsparing self-analysis for it is we who have summoned Anne Carson into being as the mimetic ground of our desire for the panoptic, that is, as the reflex of our hankering for the speech, the experience, the knowledge, the confidence and the authority of others rather than the proving and authenticating of our own. To say it differently: Carson writes on litmus paper which tells us who and what *we* are, acid sceptics or base encomiasts, scoffers or claquers. But for the most part, who and what we are – the majority of us, at any rate – is not difficult to determine. We are patchwork creatures without genuine moral and intellectual substance, preference machines lusting for unmerited approval, media constructs even in the privacy of our being. We have become dabblers in poetry and classical scholarship without having to know much about either. And Anne Carson is our reflection in a distorting mirror which is at the same time wholly accurate and orthogonal. We have appropriated her as she seems to have appropriated others. One might even say that Anne Carson is the higher Oprah. The projection of our unearned selves, she is watched, admired, and subsidized by us until reverse osmosis sets in and we are inevitably absorbed by our own emanation. Eventually we all appear on her program.[3]

In her 'Decreation: An Opera in Three Parts', Carson unintentionally explains in the concluding chorus exactly what the dilemma is:

> *Brittle failure occurs*
> *of course*
> *when the stress on a material exceeds its*
> *tensile force …*

although it is also true that

> *Brittle failure theory may*
> *in the end fail*
> *to explain how true love can*
> *ever avail*

> *against forgery.*

More to the point – recalling Celan's remark above – forgery appears to prevail rather easily over true love, true hands, true poems, and goes some distance toward explaining why such poems as we are considering may be described as brittle failures. There is nothing there, really, neither substance nor technique, to withstand the pressure of the world which every good poem both resists and turns to its advantage as it presses back against the world to modify and eventually to enter it. Instead we are furnished with exempla of what Keats described as 'the egotistical manufacture of metaphysical importance upon trivial themes'. As for the putative wit of the Decreation piece, it is, I'm afraid, painfully derivative. The central pun on forgery in connection with Hephaistos in his smithy (Part One is called 'Love's Forgery') cooled to a clinker almost a century ago with the famous peroration of Joyce's *Portrait*.

How, then, to explain her surging popularity? Might this have something to do with the current obsession with fragments and simulacra? In an age where continuity and seamlessness, artisanal craftsmanship and wholeness of original conception are at a discount, Carson writes an IKEA-type poetry, fitting together bits and pieces into a mental furniture that appears weirdly functional but is utterly devoid of charm, staying-power and liveability. It is, in effect, a poetry of screws, hinges, dowels, thin linear splines and sharp corners, a line from Akhmatova here, a *soupçon* of Celan there, little bits of Beckett and Bataille, a dollop of Plato, a generous helping of Keats, all put together according to a blueprint from Sappho. And in fact, it is no accident that some of Carson's more recent endeavours involve yet one more translation of Sappho (her newest work is called *If Not, Winter: Fragments of Sappho*) whose literary remnants tally perfectly with Carson's inclination to compose in minims and slivers slotted together and which, more importantly, correspond with the staccato temper and disjointedness of the *Zeitgeist*. What we are getting is a poetry whose composition is a function of shrewd outsourcing and subsequent importation for the mechanical assembly of parts. Alluding to Carson's self-admitted desire to give her poems the quality the Greeks called *charis* (charm, grace), Mark Scroggins in an article for *Parnassus* (vol. 26, no. 2) sensibly asks, 'What sorts of 'charm' – if any – is Carson able to conjure out of her shards of language and emotion?' The question, of course, is rhetorical.

Indeed what we are getting is a poetry that is almost impossible to satirize or deflate for the pre-emptive reason that such poems read chiefly like parodies of themselves or like the products of a sophisticated literary prank. The material has forestalled the doubter who would come to grips with it, stealing the thunder of the litigant like certain bizarre physiognomies that are the bane of the caricaturist since they render him dispensable. In this respect Anne Carson could just as well be Anne Knish who, along with Emanuel Morgan, figured as one of the two main principals in the celebrated Spectra hoax perpetrated by Witter Bynner and Arthur Davison Ficke in the early part of the last century. Of course, what Bynner and Ficke had in mind was (in the words of William Jay Smith in his book on the subject) to clear the air of 'the stuffiness that tends to gather about literature when it loses its sense of humor and earnest but lumbering personalities take over'.

But what happens when the apparent parody is not deliberate, when what properly seems like a spoof is intended seriously, when, as Smith complains, 'the element of common sense, which should shape all judgement, is … in eclipse'? To reset this question in exemplary terms, I would suggest that the following poem by one Anne ('Opus 76') could be readily mistaken for a typical poem by the other.

> Years are nothing;
> Days alone count;
> These, and the nights.
> I have seen the grey stars marching,
> And the green bubbles in wine,
> And there are gothic vaults of sleep.

Portions of the Spectra manifesto attributed to 'Anne Knish' provide the theoretical undertacking for such splintered reflections. For example, the Spectrist poem 'speaks to the mind of that process of diffraction by which are disarticulated the several colored and other rays of which light is composed.' To answer my own question, what happens when bathos takes over is that 'the pleasure of the text' is reduced to a condition of pedantic earnestness – 'My task is to carry secret burdens for the world,' Carson writes in *Short Talks* – and genuine poetic delight is relegated to the Pliocene of the discipline as the spectral Emanuel Morgan, filled with paleontological insight, deposes in a verse that challenges our critical acuity in more ways than one:

> Fun
> Is the mastodon
> Vanished complete …

\* \* \*

When writing about poets like my present subject one runs the risk of candour sounding like dyspepsia or defamation. For what it's worth, I do not consider Carson a ghostly mutant skull witch, only as a very ordinary writer of lenten inspiration who looked the wrong way – but also as a literary Autolycus of debatable taste and promotional cunning. The important question is not 'Is she really that good?' but 'Are we really that dumb?' She certainly has a kind of talent, but it seems an aposematic talent for mimicry and camouflage. *So perhaps it is not as much Carson I am objecting to as that 'gullible' readership, deluded by a spectral coloration, which is responsible for her election.* As Christopher Hitchens contends with respect to Mother Teresa in *The Missionary Position*, the argument is not so much with the deceiver as the deceived: 'If Mother Teresa is the adored object of many credulous and uncritical observers, then the blame is not hers, or hers alone. In the gradual manufacture of an illusion, the conjurer is only the instrument of the audience.' Anne Carson and Mother Teresa appear to have a lot in common – including the 'enormous weight of received opinion' on their side, a weight, as Hitchens concludes, 'made no easier to shift by the fact that it is made up, quite literally, of illusion'.

A recent example of the abject surrender of critical taste and independent literary judgement is the choir of hallelujahs that have greeted Carson's verse novella *The Beauty of the Husband*, arranged in 29 chapter-units called 'Tangos'. As Robert Potts summarizes in the *Guardian* for January 26, 2002, 'What differentiates this self-pitying account of marital unhappiness from a slice of confessional-style realism is an occasional (and occasionally clichéd) lyricism, some fashionable philosophising, and an almost artless grafting-on of academic materials … [T]he book fails as poetry, simply because it shows either crashing inability or an unbecoming contempt for the medium.'

To get to the last pages of Carson's latest mélange, we still have to dance through those 29 'Tangos'. Too many. Decently compressed and tucked into the featureless prose that is its natural medium, *Husband* would make a tidy little article on marital infidelity in *Chatelaine*. There we might better sympathize with a helplessly patient Griselda being given the terpsichorean runaround by her cynical and devilishly handsome husband. Readers with a fondness for Canadian literature might even remember the passage from Timothy Findley's *Pilgrim* (1999), in which a stricken Emma Jung, paralysed by the intellectual beauty of her philandering husband, answers his leading question: '"*If you could dance with the devil, which rhythm would you choose?" ... "The Tango,"* she would have said.' And experience the *frisson* of recognition.

In its present form, a narrative flatness stretches interminably over nearly 150 pages, glib imagistic *non sequiturs* proliferate ('He would fill structures / of threat with a light like the earliest olive oil.' But what is a *structure* of threat? and in the gender context of this 'fictional essay,' olive oil makes sense only if it signifies Popeye's girlfriend. Or is there a sleeping pun on virgin?), the clichés cluster round a central emptiness like the golden emerods of the Lord ('a raw picking wind,' 'Is innocence just one of the disguises of beauty?' 'Madness doubled is marriage.' 'You know how beauty makes sex possible.' 'Well life has some risks. Love is one.' 'But it all comes round / to a blue June moon' – not the phrase, which is intended ironically, but the irony itself is flagrantly clichéd). A hollow sententiousness echoes sepulchrally throughout: 'To stay human is to break a limitation.' Exactly. For an instance of how the subject of a disintegrating relationship may be handled poetically with genuine verbal artistry, while at the same time breaking the limitation of an established form, don't be fooled by this coy yet pedestrian verse steeped in retro-riffage and catchy doo-wah choruses. See George Meredith's *Modern Love.*

The trouble is that Carson and her admirers constitute a salient and representative phenomenon, being the latest and most conspicuous instalment in the saga of aesthetic tastelessness, derivativeness, institutional bad writing, critical stupefaction and quasi-intellectual self-promotion that (dis)qualifies the literary climate we are living in. The poetry it offers us is the DOA poetry of Flatman whose world costs 'only $2 to view/at first', before, as Carson herself informs us in the ensuing passage of the poem, the cost goes up: $37 for the book I just purchased – which on second thought may be worth the price, if only to meet such serendipitously apt lines as 'My voice is flat, my walk is flat, my ironies/move flatly out to sock you in the eye' ('Flatman [first draft]').

In essence, then, the poetry Carson and her congeners write or advocate is a poetry without verbal élan and – this is a dead giveaway – *without music,* that is, without the distinct cantabile quality, the deep and insinuating hypo-rhythm that one hears in any genuine poem, like the 'potato potato' sound of an idling Harley. 'Poetry atrophies when it gets too far from music,' said Pound, rightly. How a poet can live at so great a distance from the pitch and swing of the language, churning out line after line of largely unscannable verbiage, is one of the marvels of the performance, like that of a déclassé Swinburne for whom once, notwithstanding the disrepute into which his work has fallen, 'the tidal throb of all the tides ke[pt] rhyme'. Better the tidal throb, I submit, than the static amphidrome. David Ward again: 'Carson's lines remain brittle, short, snapped-off, and unmusical' – although of late the lines have grown longer without sacrificing their unmusicality.[4] So the reader remains stuck to the page in the instant of passive identification with what is really an inert piece of language. Nothing changes. Everything remains as is, here as elsewhere: simulated poems, imitation poets, replicant readers. And of course, the complement of friendly critics, those willing sherpas of Mount Parnassus.

Such is the condition of poetry at the present cultural juncture. The drive to produce and eulogize poems that contain scarcely a pellet of interesting or discernible content, the slightest hint of cohesive form, the rorty-sounding pulse of the language or the merest geode of a memorable phrase now seems virtually undeflectable. Such work, like the poor bedraggled bird in Carson's *New Yorker* poem (March 24, 2003), just 'grinds on, / grinds on, thrusting against black.' And it is accompanied by a lugubrious and portentous solemnity of spirit, a sort of carsonoma in both poet and reader, that augurs poorly for the recrudescence of aesthetic taste, critical judgement and verbal liveliness. 'Nothing guiding it, bird beats on.' It is truly astounding how the deficits of quality I am treating of here can be toggled into press success and canon presence, but I console myself by remembering that the quickless Reverend Bowles was, if not the most influential, arguably the most celebrated poet of *his* day and certainly one of the most ubiquitous.

And that is precisely the trouble with Anne Carson, namely, she keeps turning up everywhere you look, yet, like a variant of Hitchcock's defunct protagonist in *The Trouble with Harry*, is poetically moribund in spite of her apparent mobility. The artificiality and deadness of the poetry are palpable, relying as it does on the fake austerities of a kind of classical kitsch, like *nouvelle cuisine* presenting its sparse materials abruptly juxtaposed and elaborately done up – plate after plate of it. But don't expect this to stop an inexorable progress toward stardom fostered by a sort of critic-and-peer collusion, a veritable conspiracy of literary dunces who, loving the things they love for what they aren't, engage in the promotion of incompetents. Is there any other way to account for the latest embarrassment, Daniel Mendelsohn's lengthy, meandering article in *The New York Review* (August 14, 2003) on sundry matters Sapphic, segueing into Carson's *If Not, Winter*? Mendelsohn momentarily deprecates 'the strange waffling that characterizes her new book' which, if I follow his tentative drift, tends to lose itself somewhere in fly-over land between scholarship and impressionism; at the same time, before he finds himself in really deep doodoo, he makes sure to ring the usual carillons about Carson's learning, brilliance and originality, effectively drowning out his hesitations.

Thus is the unprepossessing griffined into lush celebrity, the wren posing as an eagle and the neutered Siamese as a lion. 'Where's probity in this' asks Geoffrey Hill in *Canaan*, 'the slither-frisk / to lordship of a kind?' Given her emblematic status, I wouldn't be at all surprised to find Anne Carson, who is not so much a poet as a prize-reaping machine, nominated for *every* award known to man or woman. Remember: you read it here first.

---

1. What I refer to in text as the 'conceptual reification' of 'Nothing' is the scholarly form of what philosophers call a 'category mistake' – if, that is, it is not a piece of scholarly dissimulation. The *semantic* distinction between upper and lower case letters dates from the Hellenistic period and in particular from the scribal culture of Alexandria when the difference began to be treated as meaningful and systematic. The Greek word for 'nothing' (*mithen*, μηδεν), still in current demotic usage, cannot in the Simonidean context be rendered as an equivalent for a later ontological abstraction. That is, with respect to early Greek thought, 'Nothing' is not and cannot be construed as a dimension of Being or a metaphysical object except under the sign of chronological legerdemain seeking to assert a backwards compatibility which the cultural facts do not warrant. Of course, in early Greek 'texts' all letters tend to appear in majuscule, but the point is that the distinction we are considering here would not register for Simonides, Heraclitus and Parmenides as it did for Celan, Heidegger and Sartre. (I am indebted to conversation with poet and essayist Yiorgos Chouliaras who addressed these

notions in a colloqium entitled *How to Be Greek*, convened at the City University of New York in 1987.)

2. The vowelled conclusion of the poem, which in the German text is rendered 'I-i-e', is most likely a scream, which commentators do not seem to hear, being among those who, as Celan lamented, 'overlook what's happening around us and do not hear the scream that never falls silent'. Or if they do hear it, they refuse to acknowledge its echo, as James Lasdun recalls in a poem entitled 'Deathmeadow Mountain' (from *Landscape with Chainsaw*), reprising – with clear attribution – John Felstiner's account of Celan's famous meeting with Heidegger. Celan signs the philosopher's guest book,

> in hope
> of a 'word in the heart'
> from the Secret King of Thought,
> the *Meister*, who withheld it
> till the poet gave up.

The penultimate line's allusion to Celan's best-known poem 'Deathfugue' is entirely chilling and apt. *[D]er Tod ist ein Meister aus Deutschland*, writes Celan, 'death is a master from Germany.'

3. A case in point: poet Sonnet L'Abbé, a contributor to the *Globe and Mail*'s weekly 'How Poems Work' section (March 2, 2002), cannot refrain from pretending that she is Anne Carson writing about her own work. The analysis of a fragment of Carson's 'TV Men' reads like a spastic reproduction of the poem itself, concluding:

> anne / the man / bo ban / name game / word game / mind games /
> all's fair in love and / osama / cnn / tv men /
> motherdaughter, copy that, I'm reading you loud and
> The shattered mirror has begun to reflect itself!

4. Carson's prosody in *The Beauty of the Husband* is praised by poet Sarah Maguire in a letter to the *Guardian* for January 4, 2002: 'The form of Carson's poem,' she instructs us, 'is borrowed from the tango's dangerously complex duet. It is the long, sinuous strides of that dance, alternated with its fast, short

bursts of action, that give *The Beauty of the Husband* its formal template of long, then short, lines.' Obviously Maguire has forgotten that the long/short linear structure, known as the epode, was first introduced by Archilochus, who played with trimeter/dimeter rotations, back in the pre-tango seventh century B.C., was then picked up by Horace, and has since become a fixture of prosodic tradition. It has continued to surface in many different ways, as for example in the poulter's measure popular in sixteenth-century English poetry, which alternated hexameters and heptameters, putting in this case the shorter line first. James Merrill's 'Octopus' exhibits one of the most intelligent uses of the epode in contemporary verse and repays close study by anyone interested in domesticating the form.

As for the tango concept itself, Timothy Steele tells the story of the dangerous dance as it inserts itself into human affairs, so to speak, far more effectively in his 'Last Tango', with its sense of Brandoesque inevitability:

> All life conspires to define us,
> Weighing us down with who we are,
> Too much drab pain. It is enough
> To make one take sides with
> Plotinus …

# DOUBLE EXILE
# AND MONTREAL
# ENGLISH-LANGUAGE
# POETRY

> And what's the news you
> carry – if you know?
> And tell me where you're off
> for – Montreal?
>
> – Robert Frost, 'An Encounter'

IT IS NO ACCIDENT that some of the best writing in English Canada is to be found in Montreal and that some of the finest poets in the entire country reside and work within a radius of a few blocks of one another. Michael Harris, Carmine Starnino, Robyn Sarah and Peter Van Toorn have lived 'in town' from the very beginning of their literary careers. Eric Ormsby moved to Montreal from the U.S. in 1986 to take up the post of Director of Libraries at McGill University and Norm Sibum, a longtime resident of Vancouver (via Germany and Alaska), arrived only a few years past but has since become an integral contributor to the poetic revival fermenting in the city. Stephanie Bolster, another recent arrival, has settled in nicely. Charlotte Hussey is associated with the very streets of Montreal – an early collection is entitled *Rue Sainte Famille* – and Robert Allen appeared on the scene in the mid-seventies via Cornell to join the teaching staff at Concordia University and eventually to assume the editorship of the literary magazine *Matrix*. Bruce Taylor arrived in 1978 and although he has recently moved to the countryside continues to regard himself, in his own words, as 'a Montreal poet if I am anything'.

The reason for so dense a concentration of virtuosity has to do with a civic and municipal condition that I call the 'double exile', a function of our peculiar demography. I refer to the fact that the small cadre of anglophone poets in Montreal is doubly cut off from an appreciative or at least available readership since it constitutes only a tiny insular minority in the midst of a sea of five million French speakers (who pay little attention to works in the 'other' language). At the same time French literature is itself a minority phenomenon surrounded on every side by a nation of twenty-five million English speakers (who, for political reasons, will subsidize its token presence but without understanding or familiarity – while ignoring the anglophone remnant almost completely). What this means for English Montreal poets, distinct from both their franco-Québécois as well as anglo-Canadian counterparts, is that they form the literary wing of a twofold hostage community. Their voices are heard neither in Quebec City nor in Toronto, a twin-barrelled neglect which leaves them in their various cummings and Gioia, whether solitary or gregarious by nature, talking pretty much to themselves, to their predecessors, to posterity or to the Lord.

The odd thing is that this relative segregation has by no means been an unmitigated disaster. Quite the contrary. For some time now it has brought along with it certain inestimable advantages from which these poets have profited as *writers* though obviously not as celebrities. Unlike their peers in the rest of the country whose work is publicized and aggressively circulated and who group together to safeguard the perks they enjoy and to collect ideological pogey, these Montreal writers have worked in substantial isolation not only from the various nationally syndicated poetries at large – the West Coast school, the Prairie School, the Southern Ontario school, the Torontocentric school, and so on – but also *from one another.* Especially with regard to diction and prosody, the private shaping of a public medium has led to genuine originality.

In other words, this state of binary preterition has created an environment in which individual poets are free to choose their own sources, influences, usage, directions and identities, reaping what we might call benefit of ostracism to build their home *in the domain of language itself,* each in his or her own special manner. Lack of public attention has liberated them from the need or the tendency to affiliate themselves with political and regional ideologies in order to further their (nonexistent) careers, a providential disregard which has sponsored a renewed sense of the printed voice and kept its possessors in touch with the free vagrancies of mind that consolidate a signature.

In this way place has been displaced into language, which becomes not simply an agency of communication but both a patrimony and an embodiment. To live in Montreal is now tantamount, for the best of these poets, to moving about fully and jubilantly in the language they explore, construct, reassemble and ultimately dwell in. Where you live has in their case become what you say and how you say it: locality disappears and re-condenses as a dialect of thought. Having absorbed the reality of exile into their inmost selves and consequent practice – having had, so to speak, autonomy thrust upon them – each of these poets has developed a distinctive style and idiolect that resists co-optation by a collective. Language has become a house with many mansions.

I give several titles as evidence for my claim. Peter Van Toorn's *Mountain Tea*, the sizzling pyrolalia of a master wordsmith in his element, is in a class by itself; nothing like it has ever been published in this country. Michael Harris's *Grace* and *In Transit* represent the kind of work that Ted Hughes would have wanted to write had he been able to. (I have long maintained that Harris is a better poet than his beloved mentor.) *For a Modest God*, as has been noted by more than one reviewer, displays the verbal gemminess of Hart Crane and the meditative sweep of Wallace Stevens, but is entirely Eric Ormsby: it stands as one of the major poetic achievements of the decade in English-language poetry. His latest book, *Araby*, is perhaps even more impressive. *Questions about the Stars* by Robyn Sarah and *The November Propertius* by Norm Sibum share few thematic and prosodic features, yet the former in its technical self-assurance and the latter in its elegiac harkening are equally *classical* productions. Robert Allen's best book of poetry might well be his novel *Napoleon's Retreat*, a veritable *tour de force* of poetic prose, and Charlotte Hussey's latest divan of versicles, *Sonnets for Zöe*, improves on her already fine, partly *montréalais* collection. Stephanie Bolster was honoured with a Governor General's Award for *White Stone: The Alice Poems* and Bruce Taylor won the QSPELL Poetry Prize for *Cold Rubber Feet* and again for his most recent collection, *facts*. Finally, *Credo*, Carmine Starnino's second book, with its innovative sixteen-part sequence 'Cornage', has brought him early and justified acclaim: 'he may in fact be the true heir to the Montreal tradition of poetic excellence,' writes one critic in a recent review.

The work, then, is *uniformly* accomplished, and yet nothing could be more *different* one from the other than the verses of Ormsby, Harris, Sarah, Sibum, Van Toorn, Allen, Hussey, Bolster, Taylor and Starnino, all of whom *as poets* could just as well be living on different planets (although some of them, it must be admitted, are fellows of the Jubilate Circle). They will meet often, of course, to discuss, argue, compare and disagree, as a talented and amicable community of independent poets whose mutual influence, while occasionally technical or prosodic, is emphatically social and personal. That is, they reinforce each other in their reciprocal and productive solitudes but stay resolutely clear of the schools and movements, the topographical identities, cultic franchises and power politics that constrain and obviate the work of the scribbling classes in other parts of the country. And while they may, as I have said, engage occasionally in mutual critique, they stay pretty well out of one another's work. The result is that the imaginative flora and fauna are different here and in some instances almost wholly singular, so that what we are seeing is the literary equivalent of Australian evolution. This is just another way of saying that these poets are not, properly speaking, Canadian (or Australian). They are merely unique.

But English Montreal, as we have seen, is in many respects a small and lonely city despite its exotic aura, 'over four centuries of cobblestones/sequined with bottle caps,' as Hussey puts it. Besieged by two generations of neglect, it has thus forced its writers in upon themselves in a kind of literary quarantine. This state of affairs, as I have argued, has compelled a number of the poets to shape their own distinctive and indelible styles, which of course does not necessarily alleviate a feeling of oppression or misprision. Opportunity permitting, there is always the temptation either to leave the premises entirely for a distant arboretum, as did Leonard Cohen in the late sixties, or to establish a defensive huddle in order to create a 'culture of belonging', a doctrinal and theoretical shelter from the storm of indifference and rejection impacting from the rest of the country.

Indeed this latter option was adopted in the seventies by the first Véhicule school of pseudo-demotic poets. Affecting the open-ended poetics of the Black Mountain bunch as it filtered through the West

Coast anagrammatic TISH movement, a byke of these early Véhiculists unleashed what seemed to many observers a veritable haemorrhage of forgettable books. The bleeding stopped in time to save these poets for other careers as pedagogues, editors and Canadianists. Finally, after a brief interregnum, an abused Véhicule Press was brought under more enlightened editorship, restored to health and reinvented, in part under the Signal Editions imprint, to be what it is today: a home for a select group of poets who have nothing in common except an abiding passion for a rigorous Muse and a refusal to share an aggregate, homogenizing poetics. The lesson, long in the learning, had been well learned.

Regrettably but perhaps inevitably, the managerial sensibility of the *initial* Véhicule movement still carries on as the Blue Metropolis annual literary symposium, in which some of the same old names tend to resurface administratively or to orbit those of the invitees, putting in effect the wrong Montreal on the map – the one that hankers for international vetting and cachet. (When Michael Harris was improbably invited to give a brief reading, he was plaided among the clan of visiting Scottish poets. Ditto Carmine Starnino who found himself renationalized as an Italian.) The festival is in the business of borrowing prestige, which it repays in the usual provincial fashion with adulation and cash – a superannuated Norman Mailer receives $10,000 to make an appearance (accompanied by a wife with literary ambitions of her own) and local media types are dewy-eyed over the prospect of interviewing Margaret Drabble, of all people. John Ashbery, whose reputation is in strictly inverse proportion to his means, becomes a little more affluent too, as does a wizened Susan Sontag, a writer long past her best days. Put a Yank or a Brit in their midst – even if, to cite a line of Rob Allen's, they are 'played out, done in, defunct' – and the festival organizers and fellow travellers circle round and round in noisy excitement like fourteen doves spooked by a cabbage white. The spectacle of so much spurious activity and obsequious gratitude is truly chastening.

The occasional quality writer who does turn up from elsewhere (like Mavis Gallant or Maryse Condé, for example), merely accentuates the general lack of spark and animation. Obviously one never gets any of this from local media outlets, which have united in touting the festival as unfailingly exciting, glitzy and *mondial* – the typical boosterism of the parochial mindset unaware of where its real strength lies. Thus it makes some sense to say that there are really two Montreals in competition with one another: the burgravial, agenda-dominated camarilla of movers and shakers connected with Blue Metropolis as well as with a cliquish outfit misnomered as the Quebec Writers Federation and the party of excellence associated with Signal Editions and the Jubilate Circle, the one denying the condition of exile and the other turning it to advantage. But it is to be expected that the former will continue to attract more attention from the media and to promote its version of what passes for a literary event for some considerable time to come.

Yet such is merely the institutional form of a cultural mediocrity whose half-life is at least as long as literature itself and must be regarded as an ineluctable feature of any literary landscape where, as Bruce Taylor writes in 'The Slough', 'all poor beasts that flit or thud / lie down with the frogs in the lathered mud.' After all, it is only natural that Montreal, like any other place, should harbour its complement of mavens and speculators as it does its quota of weak and even catastrophic poets but this is an unavoidable deficit in the creative budget of the race as a whole. And certainly it needs to be acknowledged that the city even at its best does not enjoy an absolute monopoly on good poetry. One will find a sprinkling of first-rate poets here and there beyond the gates of what Cohen once called 'a holy city … the Jerusalem of the North.'[1]

But the fact nevertheless persists. Canadian poetry has been flashing 18:88 for a long time now, probably since 1888 if not before, with brief but timely and providential returns to the world in the Montreal twenties with the *McGill Fortnightly Review*, in the forties with *Preview* and *First Statement* and now again at the turn of the century, the city enjoying perhaps an even greater distribution of genuine talent than before. The power is there if we only knew where to look. Thus, as I have not scrupled to stress and reiterate, there is little doubt that in Canada at the present time, most poetry of value, interest and consequence is being written and/or published in Montreal, which thanks to the cohort of brilliant poets and editors who have gathered here is experiencing the spirit of renewal and invigoration once again, as it did when A. M. Klein, Louis Dudek, P. K. Page, Frank Scott, Irving Layton, A. J. M. Smith, John Sutherland, Patrick Anderson and John Glassco commanded the stage.[2] Liberated from the trammels of program, region and coalition, our best editors are both stringent and encyclopedic while the poets writing here and now in the 'tradition of excellence' are those who have expanded the linguistic and architectonic spectrum, permitting themselves to use all the crayons in the box instead of just a few favourite colours like narrative yellow or confessional rust, the mainstays of what we might call the Group of Seven Million in this country. While remaining members of the larger community, the Montreal poets have gone their own way with astonishing originality. Perhaps what we are seeing at work is, *mutatis mutandis*, a specialized instance of what Charles Taylor means by 'deep diversity', each of these poets being 'a bearer of individual rights in a multicultural mosaic', that is, belonging to a common entity while hewing to a heteronymous sense of his or her own specific identity. (Or alternatively, they may be understood as operating in what poet Campbell McGrath calls 'prism[s] of refractive solitude.')

The poets I have magic-markered are the real thing, writers whose work, like Ormsby's garden snake, 'silvers the whole attention of the mind', or like Van Toorn's mountain heron, refuses to be deflected from its purpose, 'Still fishing the lake, / same spot – after all that rain.' These are writers who can hold their own with and even surpass the achievement of their more celebrated contemporaries anywhere in the world – though it may take yet another generation before the truth comes to light. We will then have to figure out some way of expiating our lack of acumen and maturity and rendering due justice.

Meanwhile, the state of double exile – a paradoxical condition of twice solitary yet richly communal productivity – has unexpectedly turned out to be a creative godsend for which the more cuddled poets in Victoria and Calgary and Toronto, if they had an eye to permanence and an ear for Promethean language, might well envy their Montreal counterparts.

---

1. The Maritime provinces might also make a strong case for themselves as a centre of genuine poetic creativity – what with poets like Brent MacLaine, Ross Leckie, Geoffrey Cook and Mary Dalton – but I leave it to others to account for the reasons. There are also encouraging signs from elsewhere, such as the recent work of Elise Partridge, Ken Babstock and John O'Neill. Let us hope.

2. I cannot resist customizing the first part of a celebrated Wordsworth poem to suggest what the city at a privileged period in its literary history has given us:

> Great men have been among us: hands that penned
> And tongues that uttered wisdom – better none:
> The early Dudek, Klein and Sutherland,
> Young Cohen, and others who called Layton friend.

# DOUGIE'S ANGELS

TOWARD THE END of *Charlie's Angels* the camera pans on Dylan, Natalie and Alex along with their sidekick Bosley heading for a spirited romp along the beach. Tomboy, dancer, exotic and friend are celebrating a good day's work. The villain has been blown to smithereens, literally hoist on his own rocket-powered petard; Charlie is still in benevolent control; the three angels are as winsomely limber as ever; and Bosley (played by Bill Murray, not George, although the resemblance is striking) is his charming and genial self as he struggles manfully to keep up with the girls.

Analogously, though in a somewhat more intellectually upscale dimension, Doug Gibson, president and publisher of McClelland and Stewart, has just dispatched three angels and one companion into the world of Canadian poetry to shake things up and put matters right. These are for the most part accessible writers who, I suspect, will inspire affection and solicitude in their readers. And indeed, some are capable of interesting verbal effects from time to time, and one is even a very good poet.

\* \* \*

Less than two years after publishing a clearly unfinished manuscript, Shawna Lemay has catapulted onto the set again with *Against Paradise*, which resembles its predecessor in being equally premature. What's the hurry? one wants to ask. Is the world about to end, compelling us to make our mark before it is too late? Poetry is perhaps the loneliest and most time-dependent of all the arts, requiring years of solitary application, a slow and laborious process of intense cultivation, and the patience to wait for serendipitous arrivals and unforeseen ripenings. I make these remarks at the outset because Lemay is representative of many of her contemporaries in displaying precisely the lack of patience, the unwillingness to wait upon experience and to focus minutely on matters of craftsmanship, that is responsible for the deep doldrums in which poetry finds itself today.

Her intention in *Against Paradise* is to scroll her way around the historical circumference of Venice and penetrate gradually to its lurid, theatrical interior, telling its story the way her own George Sand would need 'a year of perfume, clouds and solitude' in order to relate 'th[e] story of a teacup properly'. But the problem is that the desire to kern the interval between books to ensure the poet's overall 'readability' as a public figure is reflected in the dishevelled and undisciplined quality of the work itself. So we get reams of lines and passages strewn about helter-skelter like clothes across Dylan's floor:

> I perch in the frangible ecstasy
> of shadow and delight
> in the savage quivering ...

or

> skirt design
> and flee, femme fatale
> slough that cryptic cryogenic gold
> slither
> drag that magic carpet ...

Much of the time, I must confess, I have no idea what Lemay is talking about. How can a throne 'sink into fractured air'? Why does every dream come up with a burning map and a glass of water? Tell me more about those 'inexpressible stomach/orgies.' And where the writing does happen to be intelligible, it often runs to little more than a kind of *talking on the page*, a loose and garrulous spill of not particularly memorable words tracing, for example, 'scenes of domestic bliss/long unravelled' or commenting that on the 'Day before departure/there is a total eclipse of the sun lasting one hour.' This sort of thing is pervasive but what it has to do with poetic language and architectonic shaping remains an insoluble mystery. The higher Baedeker at best.

Like the Venetian days Lemay describes, these poems are 'tangled

68

and ripe/with insignificance'. If you want to embark on an imaginative excursion into an emblematic Venice, you're better off accompanying, among recent adventurers, Robert Coover in *Pinocchio in Venice* or Joseph Brodsky in *Watermark*. At least you'll know where you've been.

\* \* \*

As *A Strange Relief* is a first collection, one cannot arraign its author for ambitious haste. What Sonnet L'Abbé has going for her, apart from her marvellous name (only Lake Sagaris, zAyla weedz and Crystal Hurdle come close to such onomastic dazzle) is the capacity to pay out a line tractably across the page and over a lengthy sequence of enjambments. This reflects a certain tenacity of thought that is quite rare in a time of multiple distraction and short-term memory. The poems *seem* meditated and unhurried, accreting slowly line by line like her own 'geologic argument' in 'Lesson from the Neolithic Era', where with 'abrasive persistence' and considerable adroitness she heaves her metamorphic strata from sea to land. 'Winter Olympics' offers a good example of such artisanal flexibility of means which, once sustainable, will furnish this poet with a firm technical foundation on which to build.

> You must pretend
> > the judges aren't a row
> of reluctant suitors, sixes
> > tucked behind their backs like too-
> expensive rings ...
> > A voice from above
> calls your name. Skate out
> > into the ellipse of light, opal of frost.
> Freeze into the figure
> > of a cake-top ballerina, wait for the first note ...

And yet, regrettably, there is a manifest tendency to cliché and to the flat declarative that suggest the poet would have been better served to defer publication until such evident defects were attended to. 'The secret of beauty is all around us,' we are informed. 'Realize this: a circle is describable,' we are told. 'True kings discard influence,' we are further enlightened. There seems no end to these Polonians. 'What we make of living/is remembered only by the living.' 'It is not/adultery, but getting caught/that costs.' Such pseudo-aphoristic mackles are always a little disquieting in a poet's work, as if they were, to cite L'Abbé herself from 'The Potter's Daughter',

> flaws
> discovered in the final firing,
> sometimes the unpredicted
> source of beauty, but more often
> ruinous, incalculable errors,
> forcing the same work
> redone from the beginning.

Similarly, what looks at first like a gift for apt comparison starts to grow worn and wobbly once she lets her vigilance slip, which is often. Then we discover that the lights of Toronto 'sparkl[e]' like 'facets of yellow jewels reflected/in calm water' or that 'the human mind is beautiful as numbers.' Nor does the conspicuous effort at cleverness rescue these pieces from the sag of homiletic platitude. To read that the moth 'burns/to throw itself/into fire', to hear our servant horses tell us 'we ate out of your hands,' and to find in the backwards count of the anaesthetist a 'valediction promising morning' with its creaky allusion to Donne's 'A Valediction: Forbidding Mourning', merely tax the reader's forbearance unduly. One thinks of the groan that accompanies the too-insistent pun and recalls that poetry cannot survive long on readerly concession.

Regardless of the technical nimbleness one detects here and there and occasional instances of phrasal crispness, there are simply not enough such moments to indemnify the reader's investment of time and trust, of which we have too little to waste on the acres of casual, incomplete work clamouring loudly for our attention. Back to the dance studio. The elasticity is there. What is now needed are the diligence and seasoning.

* * *

Lorna Goodison, though rather more flamboyant than her sister angels, can scarcely be accused of sprinting into print before her time. But this does not absolve her from the charge of unwarranted prolificity when one considers: her *Selected* in 1993, *To Us All Flowers Are Roses* in 1995, *Turn Thanks* in 1999, *Guinea Woman* in 2000, and *Travelling Mercies*, the subject of our review, in 2001. Despite the blitz of publications, the glittering skein of prizes and awards (including the Commonwealth Poetry Prize in 1986 and the Nimrod International Award in 1992), and the intemperate blurbing of Nobel Laureate Derek Walcott (who finds in her poetry 'a rooted, organic delight ... fresh in its wit and pain and in the high spiritual gossip of its leaves'), one is still left to wonder how so redundant and indeed *stifling* a poet has managed to make it this far in what we once thought to be a ruthlessly competitive world.

The title poem sets the tone early, a drab prosy repetitiveness of 'language moments' that seems oddly *dubbed* into poetry rather than ringing the carillons of syllable and rhythm the back cover leads us to expect. If there is a 'ring' at all to this verse, assuming her own doggerel self-attestation,

> all the verdant valley ringing
> with coloratura converter singing,

it is the ring of a steel band playing for a party of bemused tourists. The lilt and syntax of what we are obviously meant to regard as the natural inflections of island dialect sound put on, creolized, like a kind of take-out exoticism – as if natal authority resided in lopping the definite article wherever feasible ('fly through hidden other eye'), banishing the pronoun ('Even so, is so'), decolonializing inflections ('So the converter sing'), razing the copula ('turn your key/when you private'), and plying the bizarre phrasing of the kitsch indigenous ('It's my medicine bundle, don't it?'). I guess some of us go be liking this poetry for sure-sure. The genre Goodison works in is not one that takes its origin in the alluvial mix of local speech as it pretends to – no Bunny Wailer or even much Walcott here – but may instead be characterized as a type of false verisimilitude, which is licit only if the practice is ironic and deflationary: Spike Lee in blackface. But there is little in the way of irony here.

The question I am finally left with has to do with that of simple purpose. Why did these poems need to be written or disseminated in the first place? What do we gain from learning that the reason our crossover griot 'turn poet/not even she know'? What vindicates the cascade of bad puns (the betrayer 'led eyeless to gaze,' etc.) and the columns of hackneyed phrases ('narrow as the straight road to heaven,' etc.)? Poem after poem on every conceivable minor provocation without let or hindrance may result, perhaps, in stunning the mind into temporary acceptance. But when the serial concatenations eventually subside, one may perhaps be forgiven for wondering: is any poet's life this unique, this *momentous*, that readers should surrender their own dwindling reserves of time and fortitude to accommodate its stentorian claims? As for the completed work, it will no doubt be amply rewarded by literary juries and committees for bringing poetry into even deeper disrepute than where it currently malingers.

* * *

Now where have we seen this before? George Murray's prior book came out in 2000 and his second, *The Cottage-Builder's Letter*, follows hard on its heels with a kind of cv-driven velocity. Nevertheless, Murray, like his namesake in the film, is sociable, leisurely and complaisant. He writes a measured verse, a kind of plain speech relatively untroubled by metrical considerations. Again, like Bosley, he is given to a palpable earnestness of tone and a penchant for philosophical riffing which succeeds only differentially. When he is on his game the poems work by virtue of a deceptive artlessness, hiding a complexity of metaphorical effects that insinuate themselves subtly into the memory. Writing of a couple busy 'converting' a church into a home, he captures the essence of the spirit's project in our age to render the god-abandoned world habitable, yet at the same time, shuttling between flashbacks and fastforwards, suggests the pathos of the improbable present:

> the Christ-figure
> hanging above the bell tower using the cross as a crutch
> to keep himself from falling to earth, his final moments spent
> as he always wished he could and working
> as a simple weather vane that only warns of one kind of storm.

But certain technical problems tend to arise from time to time in the course of the work. Perhaps the major predicament involves an unsure hand calibrating the relative dynamics of metaphor and simile. When the poems are doing what Murray wants them to, they operate like unit-body constructions, each with the engine of metaphor bolted solidly within and generating sufficient implicative power to move his Lexus from the writer's page to the reader's mind. But Murray sometimes forgets his own defining strength as a poet and lapses into a self-indulgent craving for overt comparison. The poems then betray a weakness for the ubiquitous preposition – hardly a line without its caper of similes, its predilection for small-time allegory.

Thus the title poem itself, divided into seven sections over ten pages, strives for *tour de force* status by arranging for almost every stanza to batter its way into existence with the common, intrusive, hammering 'like', bringing the analogical mechanism to the surface in what would seem like an effort to show off the poet's fertility of invention and to give the piece a kind of weird architectural cachet. Ah yes, as Inspector Clouseau might say, the old Pompidou Centre ploy. But once the novelty wears off, which happens by the time we reach the third section, the poem simply bogs down in a mere distraction of 'likes',

> like the nothing he can't think of telling just yet ...
> like the merciless red ants that run in the tide rills.

Murray will eventually straighten out his metaphor-simile imbroglio, and there are enough strong poems in this collection to suggest that he is heading there anyway. Pieces like 'A Good Life in the Converted Church' and 'An Egyptian Soldier on the Red Sea Swims Away from Moses' are ready for the anthologies. He has the poet's instincts, the knack for turning a good phrase and the verbal grit and suppleness to keep the reader engaged. But since nothing is assured and one may unwittingly find oneself in the path of one's own voice (to adapt a line from his Cassandra suite), a few more years innocent of publication and devoted instead to preparation would help steer an important talent toward its natural consummation. Good poetry, like good wine, needs to be *chambréd* for a spell.

* * *

To conclude with a new scenario. Let our four protagonists frisk about the beach before the story begins, not after it has ended. Let them take their time, avoid the amphetaminic hurtle into publication, and continue getting in shape for their future exploits. Whereupon they may find themselves in a position to gratify the boss's confidence more amply than has heretofore been the case and elegantly dispense with the requisite baddies, that is, with the snarly reviewers and snooty older poets who imprudently wish to advise them.

# LOUIS DUDEK:
# A PERSONAL MEMOIR

I CAN VIVIDLY RECALL when, as a sophomore at McGill in the early sixties, I saw him walk into the classroom to open the book on European Modernism, a tall, thin, scholarly-looking man who seemed a little tilted to one side as if he were listening to the conversation of a shorter world. There was an air of expectation in the room of the kind that attends a man who precedes his reputation by force of sheer presence, but without a hint of the intimidation or superiority that professorial entities often radiate. What endeared him to me most at first was his expression, which I have never forgotten and which was constantly rekindled even in his old age: a look of habitual concern and earnestness that would suddenly vanish to be replaced by the puckish grin of a clever street urchin who had just picked Shakespeare's pocket.

Allied to his unfailing courtesy, this had the effect of putting us all at our ease and turning the proceedings away from seminar seriousness toward something like a social occasion in which peers met to discuss intellectual issues. Yet we understood that we were being addressed, questioned, prompted and taught by a polymath who seemed to know incalculably more than his subject, whose lectures seemed like unrepeatable performances (except that he repeated them every week throughout the academic year, each one different from the last) and whose classes would frequently conclude to a spontaneous burst of applause.

In thinking about Dudek as a tutor and guide, 'charismatic' is not quite the right word to apply, since he could also be so appealingly modest and self-effacing. He was, in fact, the *archetypal* teacher, whose lectures one looked forward to the way one anticipates going to a movie or a play. Something was always *happening*. As his student over a period of several years, I cannot attest to a single moment of boredom. He had the art of bringing ideas to life, of drawing brilliantly apt comparisons, and of choosing illustrations from any historical period or apparently unrelated discipline. Moreover, he carried his erudition, which was encyclopedic, as casually as a Rolodex. I still remember the highlights twinkling off his glasses like little asterisks indicating the commentaries, jokes and asides with which he would sprinkle his talk. I guess what I'm trying to say is that I have never met anyone who could mix gravity and levity so effortlessly.

But his finest virtue as a teacher was his power for igniting enthusiasm, instilling in us a desire to learn and to emulate. This was not simply a pedagogical gift but a function of the lively and passionate imagination of a poet and a lover of poetry. Whether quoting whole passages from memory or lavishing anecdotes on us, he made the poets and their work seem real, even irresistible. A sizeable number of his students decided they were intended by fate to become Dante or at least Baudelaire. Nearly everyone began to write.

Fired with a partly borrowed eagerness, we tended to see our fledgling literary steps as the colossal strides of the divinely anointed. He made us feel *chosen*, as if we belonged to the circle of the elect, to Wallace Stevens' 'poetic sodality'. We felt masonic, revolutionary and indomitable. I sometimes think that I owe my present unenviable condition to Dudek for it was he, in his dual capacity of mentor and editor, who first convinced me that I had the wherewithal and stamina to become a poet. Punning on the name of the great nineteenth-century Italian master Leopardi, to whose work he initially introduced me, he said to me one day in his office after reviewing a manuscript I had submitted for commentary: 'Welcome to Leo's party.'

In later years our agendas took us to different places. His deepening involvement with Ezra Pound made his poetry seem derivative and somewhat prosy, at any rate to his newly critical ex-student. Much as I tried, I could never come to accept his long poems, *Europe*, *En México*, *Atlantis* and the *Continuations* series as anything more than the diary entries of an interesting mind. I found myself agreeing with Irving Layton that Dudek's true gift as a poet was for the lyric mode he had abandoned many years before and recollected in *Continuations I (An Infinite Poem in Progress)* as

'Putting together lyrics'

With sex, talk, contact ...

Having lost the dream, I feel no anguish
Lassitude itself is a dream

Still a happiness between the thighs, an awakening
A pleasure in the morning light

– lines that take us back almost a lifetime to the marvellous 'Pomegranate' and its 'hexagons of honey' crystallizing into lucent gems, giving off their own interior nuptial light as 'the world starts to life.' When Dudek wrote of pomegranates, he was a poet. When he wrote of infinity, I'm not sure what he was, but he was not the poet he should have and perhaps could have been.

But, to keep things in perspective, I should point out that Dudek came in time to regard my own work as disablingly conservative and neoclassical. He had published my first book, an entirely uncooked and moonstruck affair, in his McGill Poetry Series and launched my career as a stuttering and premature imagist poet in the tradition of Williams and Pound. He was, no doubt, merely trying to bolster a gosling's sense of chosenness. The result was that I found myself walking into a poetic cul-de-sac it took me nine years to work my way out of and another five or six to lay definitively to rest. It was only by going against the Dudek grain, painfully unlearning so much of what he had taught me to do *as a practising poet*, that I was finally able to arrive at my own sense of what a poem might be, but – and this bites to the core of our relationship – only with the help of the very tradition into which he had initiated me. So I gradually realized that despite our alienation I owed my former teacher a profound if troubled debt of gratitude.

As it happened, years went by without the two of us exchanging a word. Eventually we managed to bring off a tentative rapprochement in which he forgave me my apostasy and I acknowledged his right to err, the two of us as stubborn and latterly affectionate as a master teacher and a headstrong student could possibly be. Yet even during our estrangement it was always consoling to know that he was around, writing, editing, publishing, lecturing, engaging in polemics, and encouraging new writers to tempt success – which also meant to court failure – with neither arrogance nor fear, but always with conviction in the redemptive power of the imagination.

Louis Dudek was a superb teacher and an important poet. He was also a great man. His leaving diminishes us. He will be missed no less than he will be remembered.

# PLINY'S VILLA

But after vertue gan for age to stoupe,
And mighty manhode brought a bedde of ease:
The vaunting Poets found nought worth a pease,
To put in preace emong the learned troupe.
Tho gan the streames of flowing wittes to cease,
And soonebright honour pend in shamefull coupe.

> – Edmund Spenser, *The Shepheardes Calender*

The steeples are toppled
and the land unpeopled,
reclaimed by thistle
and buffalo grass.

> – Timothy Murphy, 'Buffalo Commons'

IF THE TWENTIETH CENTURY is the great age of triviality, poetry is no exception to the general contagion. There are many influential schools of modern and contemporary poetry whose effect has been to reduce the dignity and seriousness of what was once considered a calling, a vocation, a *mysterion*, to the level of a *parti pris*. Technically, modern poetry is now pretty well synonymous with free verse. Its several characteristics are observable at a glance distributed across the field of current practice: horizontal slabs, vertical flitches, or slant dribbles of print that to the layman appear gimmicky or precious; inscrutable line indentations and unmotivated line breaks (whose justification as formally mimetic is really an apology for lack of control); on occasion a funny kind of spelling its practitioners define as phonetic but which to the untrained eye resembles dyslexic kindergarten exercises or the efforts of second-language neophytes; a generous peppering of colloquial phrases and tenement idioms; the baffling absence of traceable connections between passages, stanzas or verse paragraphs where the latter can be detected, which is an aspect of the higher unintelligibility so much current verse affects; and last but not least, in the wake of Jacques Derrida's *Glas*, facing columns of text to suggest the fugal complexities of discourse but producing little more, one suspects, than hermeneutic astigmatism and the banalization of the craft. One would have to go back to the October Eclogue in *The Shepheardes Calender*, in which Spenser laments the mediocrity of the poets of the day, the dearth of noble subjects, and the pernicious influence of fashion, to find an adequate if proleptic account of the current situation.

Now there are no doubt technical and metaphysical reasons for the drab or obscurantist prosody so beloved of the moderns. One has to do with the wholesale jettisoning of the past as so much useless lumber weighing down the fragile craft of poetry tossed about in the storm of contemporary history. The forms, modes, attitudes and assumptions associated with the poetry of the past are judged inadequate to the task of expressing or surviving the horror and complexity of the present. Make It New, said Pound, looking epicanthically at the chaos around him (to which he eventually contributed himself). A democratic poetry had been born or reborn. Williams was busy publishing little prose telegrams or churning out reams of civic bombast. Cummings, despite his aristocratic *hauteur*, descended to the proletarian lower case. The Beats began breathing hard: the barrel-chested generated long, meandering, oratorical arabesques, the skinnier poets brought up choppy, blood-flecked lines that betokened suffering and disaffection. Soon the virgule became ubiquitous as Gillette. A fancy poetics evolved to explain all these shenanigans, graced by such impressive locutions as 'composition by field', 'open-ended lines', the poem as 'energy-construct', and 'the return to the body' – a pretty hard thing to leave, one would think, if you like hanging around the place. Then along came the movements stamped with official monikers like '*language* poetry' (busy 'packing the unsentence,' as Ron Silliman writes in *Tjanting*, lost somewhere in the mental desert between *not this* and *what then*) and 'performance poetry' (a kind of second-rate hip hop living only by audacity) that contested mainstream practice so effectively they soon became mainstream themselves, the new entrenched orthodoxy. The latest *trompe l'intelligence* is 'deconstruction': a fashionable poem is one that deconstructs itself, leaving the reader to wonder why it bothered to get itself constructed in the first place.

Another reason for this insurrection in what is increasingly coming to be known as postmodern poetry is the insidious and conscious presumption of the new *vates* that he is the chosen exponent of Truth, or what amounts to the same thing under another and glitzier term, the indeterminacy of Truth. The poetry of the past was largely a decorative lie, the application of verbal cosmetics to officially sanctioned, timeless themes such as love and death. Time, then, to clean out the Augean stables of the tame, tradition-bound, truth-loving Houyhnhnms nickering so ingenuously into sonnet-bags. 'Truth' or the truth that there is no 'Truth' means telling it like it is; hence street talk, uncensored expletives, slum currency, phatic utterance galore. 'Truth' means spelling it like it is; argal, yu shd rite frum th hart. But 'Truth' especially means yelling it like it is, or like you think it is; thus the poet shoves the poem aside and steps in to take its place, becoming conspicuous, infallible and obnoxious. This is even the case for the ostensibly well-mannered, modest and tactful: there is nothing more disturbing than a loud whisper.

Such is the real meaning behind the revolution (or as I have called it, the insurrection) in more or less recent poetry. There are two basic and conflicting attitudes a poet can adopt toward his or her vocation. When Yeats said, 'I am my Collected Works' and 'It is myself I revise', he meant that the poem precedes the poet. After a lifetime of serious and disciplined writing, one may, perhaps, be entitled to call oneself a poet, or one may even have to wait for the judgement of posterity rather than that of Harold Bloom or Helen Vendler. Eliot was once asked whether he was a poet and replied, 'I write verse.' Same idea. Today all this has changed. The poet precedes the poem. One is born a poet or has somehow acquired possession of that sacred and inalienable entelechy – the poet's soul, and therefore everything one writes is by definition poetry. The poetic gift, the poetic personality, the poet's imprescriptible right and genius: this is the knot in the thread, what we start with. Certainly one can take a creative writing course, or learn from resident masters, or assimilate a forensic manifesto, but this amounts to no more than perfecting the skills and honing the tools with which one is somehow – magically – equipped. I am convinced that when Marcel Duchamp signed the urinal and pronounced it thereby a work of art he was merely satirizing a presupposition that was in the process of becoming universal.

The *true* poets of the past had no time for this sort of nonsense. They were moved by the grandeur of their themes and the seriousness of their labour. Can one imagine that truly revolutionary poet, the biblical Amos, caught up in the fury of his moral indignation, pondering the effect of an indentation? Or Ezekiel, exalted by the vision of archangelic chariots, distributing slashes at appropriate places in his screed to indicate wheelspokes? One has a hard time imagining Juvenal, excoriating the follies and cruelties of Domitian's Rome, theorizing about breath units or meditating on the arbitrary and contingent nature of the Real. Would Dante, absorbed in the contemplation of the multifoliate Rose, thank heaven for this graphic and unforgettable insight into the nature of concrete poetry? Or Milton, justifying God's ways to men, thunder *ex cathedra* on dropping syllables and articles to shorten the distance between text and inspiration? Can one even conceive of Yeats or Blok or Lorca or Montale or Amichai or Milosz, who were all engaged in *important* projects, playing Lipogram? The greatest free verse poet of the modern era, Walt Whitman, carried away by his vision of America and the brotherhood of man, gave us his leaves of grass parted by a prophetic, not an intestinal, blast of thunder and wind. The reader can extend this list at will.

Fast-forwarding to the contemporary moment, we might ask where the self-indulgent and *representative* John Ashbery and his congeners, plying their flaccid and unintelligible *longueurs* to mime the operations of consciousness in an access of textual undecidability, would fit among the Parnassian elect. As Ashbery writes with bathetic accuracy in 'The Thief of Poetry',

> The snow
> that day
> blurred all but the most obtuse

– a perfect summary of our condition in the wintry climate of our poetic milieu. Similarly, Jorie Graham, who enjoys benefit of obfuscation no less than Ashbery, fills Groliers with adoring cognoscenti, none of whom understand a word she is saying – which does not prevent them from acclaiming the irrelevance of the work. But there is still, perhaps, a modicum of hope for the intermittent survival of craft, competence and corpus in what was once honoured as the *discipline* of poetry: if, that is, to cite a few resonant names, James Merrill and Philip Larkin continue to be read, if Richard Wilbur does not cease in his efforts to redeem what is rapidly becoming an increasingly banausic public Muse, if Seamus Heaney's Irish syllables keep on rubbing against one another like sociable drinkers in a cosy pub or, eschewing the misfortune of *Electric Light*, like lovers in a lamplit inn (Seems Horny is how Yevtushenko pronounced his name), if Geoffrey Hill's gnomic ohmage and Michael Harris's happy *ménage à trois* of humour, lilt and trope manage to retain the reader's attention, if Rodney Jones can survive his surprisingly turgid *Elegy for the Southern Drawl* and return to form, if Timothy Steele continues to work his customary magic summoning a compelling syntactical flow from apparently confining structures, and if Eric Ormsby's mitred passagework of sensuous detail and verbal authority is permitted to do its job in reviving the mycelial Lazarus of the word. As Paul Valéry cautioned us: 'To rely on inspiration rather than craft is to say what costs nothing is most valuable and what is most valuable costs nothing. The poet who finds his truth in mindless self-expression recommends himself to the stupidity of the reader.'

And *craft* – the sense of purpose embodied in apt words and fit structures – is the operative term here. For in a good poem even accident and chaos must be planned and orderly, or deliberately incorporated into the work, much like Pliny's villa whose garden, according to Robert Castell's *Villas of the Ancients* (1728), contained an area of irregularity called the *pratulum* (where 'nature appears in her plainest and most simple dress') and another called the *imitatio ruris* (where 'hills, rocks, cascades, rivulets, woods and buildings were thrown together in an agreeable disorder'). Without a *supervening* order and formal container, what we know as Pliny's villa could not have been built. In the same way, even the most elaborate of poems will make room for its own *pratulum* or *imitatio ruris* and, in point of fact, it is only in virtue of such formal elaboration that the presumably nonuniform may generate meaning and pleasure in the first place. In genuine poetry, the spontaneous is always an *effect*, not a condition of authenticity. The natural is a function of artifice and what we read as improvisation is carefully worked into the fabric of the poem. A finished poem is a rational construct, ideally explicable and justifiable irrespective of *both* the unconscious and impromptu properties of the initial stages of composition and the apparent, unrehearsed and extempore quality of the completed thing itself (especially to the ear). Poems are organized objects, not subjective expulsions, and even the transgression of form is, if properly conceived and handled, an aspect of form.

Robert Frost puts it with aphoristic pith and brevity in a late poem entitled 'Pertinax':

> Let chaos storm!
> Let cloud shapes swarm!
> I wait for form ...

and the fine Canadian poet Charles Bruce in 'Biography' compares the poet by implication to his farmer-protagonist who 'drilled his rows, / And planned his house and finished what he planned.' It is only in the rare case of pure and undeflectable genius that a poem may emerge seemingly worked or inevitable, its lines unblotted – but as it happens most of us do not fall into this category despite our congenial habits and assumptions.

One more thing. The enormous irony implicit in the incessant trivializing practised by our strutting postmodernist is that, far from having become humble and democratic, a man or woman among men or women, theoretically accessible to a large public, an inhabitant of what Adam Gopnick felicitously calls 'the little climate' and a metro strap-hanger like the rest, he has receded into the far and unapproachable distance. In a word, he has become, not difficult, but insignificant. It is true that poetry has fallen on hard times: the public is indifferent or uneducated or both. But when the poet starts passing off the infinitely banal as the adventurously avant-garde, when the poetry begins to read as if it were merely the illustration of an underlying poetics to which the poet clings with all the ardour of his partisan and reductive soul, then he is just compounding the felony and merits the oblivion to which he has been bluntly and unequivocally committed. And so the poet becomes the recondite and eccentric figure he claims to have superseded. The pioneers seem strangely archaic for all their fashionable pretensions.

The genuine poets, though equally unread, have at least the

satisfaction of authenticity. They remain poets not propagandists. They have not backed into the trade because they are generally incapable of useful work in some other métier or because they believe that way lies glory. They do not waste their time producing superior copy or noncupative wailings or instances of the Higher Scrabble but strive to regain the elements of a discipline long consigned to neglect or misprision, as if taking to heart the words of Chilean poet Nicanor Parra in 'The Situation Is Getting Delicate':

> I say we ought to go back ...
> The old folks were right:
> We have to go back and cook with wood again.

My point is only that if poets are moved by a great and magisterial theme, lacerated by Swiftian indignation, driven by a sincere and passionate moral fervour or consumed by a seraphic love of language, that is, if they have something *necessary* to say and the incandescent words to say it with, then they have neither the leisure nor the inclination to preoccupy themselves with the slashes, pictures, tribal chantings, energy-constructs, diary entries, lower case or indeed upper case orgies, programmatic misspellings, cryptic lacunae, grammatical syncopes, PL8SPK orthographies, chthonic rumblings and ethnopoetic whiffles, vocalic vacuums, *zaumist* irrationalities, whambam poetry slams, chunks of undigested prose, syntactic mystifications, frail little pseudo-stanzas celebrating flowers, columnar intertexts, shopping lists, Cagean mesostics or prepared piano, telepoetic effusions, interfacings of text, sound and silence, poems in four movements for three voices, central spires of longtall parts, footnotes dangling from blank space, technical and theoretical posturings *ad vomitatum*, and all the rest of what forms a considerable part of contemporary poetry whose central feature is, I'm afraid, that it is inoperable. Sad to say, but the layman is right.

# STANDARD AVERAGE CANADIAN

THE DEATH OF AL PURDY on April 21, 2000, was one of those water-shed events that mark how a culture or a nation proceeds to recognize and define itself. During the course of a long and distinguished career as a poet and chronicler of the national scene, he had come to be regarded as a quintessential Canadian, a deputy-at-large who spoke for the people and whose iconic presence reflected their multiple and composite image. So much was this the case that in mourning his depar-ture we were at the same time also celebrating our arrival. He had helped us to acknowledge ourselves and to come redeemingly to terms with who we were. And indeed, for some of his more enthusiastic followers, his death on Good Friday might have seemed curiously serendipitous.

Rarely has a poet's passing in this country generated so many eulo-gies and memorials. Purdy was lauded for his strenuous ordinariness, his heroic stature as the unpretentious common man who expressed and summarized in his work the unassuming and colloquial identity of the country, the Stompin' Tom Connors of the poetry world. As George Bowering wrote in the Copp Clark *Studies in Canadian Literature* series (quoting Doug Fetherling who had prequoted Bowering), 'He cannot help but take a lot of Canada with him. He was even so typical looking.' Revered as the genius of the local and the mundane, he 'sounded, looked, acted and thought like your imagined average Canadian to do. That's why he's so beloved,' said his publisher. He was praised by one of his more visible disciples as the greatest Canadian poet of the century who changed our poetic idiom and 'gave a younger generation of poets permission to write about anything … His was really the voice of the common man and the common woman.'

And here is precisely where we should pause and begin to reconsider. Wordsworth, we recall, in the Preface to the *Lyrical Ballads*, also canon-ized the voice of the common people but, shrewd and insightful as he was, saw to it that he did not take his own counsel seriously. The great Romantic always knew that the voice of the common man or woman is not the voice of poetry but – the voice of the common man or woman, which is exactly what the poet is when he or she is not at the writing table struggling to get something *other* than a casual conversation or a string of privy reflections down on the page. Purdy's versified report on the perils of boreal defecation, entitled 'When I Sat Down to Play the Piano,' is a good example of the latter. The poet is certainly to be credited for his chutzpah, and probably only Purdy

> surrounded by a dozen fierce Eskimo dogs
> with an inexplicable (to me) appetite
> for human excrement ...

could turn a pack of huskies snapping at the squatter's hindparts into material for 'poetry'.

But if we attend closely to the *poem*, we will see that the technique is that of mere narrative or reportage, the structure muddled and amorphous, the tone laid on with a trowel, lumberingly mock-plaintive and corny, and the language entirely unremarkable despite the coy archaism he affects ('He cometh forth hurriedly from his tent / and looketh for a quiet sequestered vale'). And therein lies the dilemma. For although the *incident* is one that we are not likely to forget, the verbal armature of the poem manages to escape retention almost perfectly, since it is the kind of language which, as Chaucer said, 'savours the less the longer it may last / By fulsomeness of its prolixity.' Purdy ends the piece with a postscript: 'Next time I'm gonna take a gun,' which is surely in the circumstance a more appropriate instrument than a pen.

Or consider in this context one of his best-known poems, 'Poem for One of the Annettes', which we pick up in the third stanza following a prior list of the various ladies in question.

> Or Janine from Poland who's
> a citizen of Canada knocked up
> in Montreal by a Yank from
> Columbus Ohio and
> > abandoned and

the abortion took place in the Town of
Mount Royal and the foetus had
no name –

Cry for your own bad judgement in
   loving him with good tears that
     will not
       fall
        but stay
in the blue beginning of every evening when
factory watchmen are coming on duty and
silent lovers are visible as moths hovering on
streetcorners
         in eccentric silver orbit
as permanent as any in
        Maisonneuve's cynical metropolis –

Cry the common sickness with ordinary tears
                As if
they would flood the whole quasi-romantic town of
Montreal with the light of your darkness and
follow the gutters and sewers glowing down
thru sewage disposal plants by the river and
into the industrial waste of your dreams to
     the sea
        the shapeless mothering one-celled sea –

Oh Anita, they do.

The tough-guy swagger and offhand vernacular that Purdy likes to
conscript into his tonal register is, according to Bowering, 'an attempt to
cover the sadness so that he not be thought sentimental.' In this particu-
lar piece, his empathy with 'the poor girl, knocked up and abandoned'
and his protest against 'man's inhuman distortion of his condition' are
supposed to justify the verbal sloppiness, the now trite oxymoron trying
to be clever ('the light of your darkness')[1] and the lack of formal control
over his materials. But no poet should revise downward to his subject if

he or she wishes to construct a lasting artifact. Rather the subject needs to be raised into the world of art, not by cleaving to a rigid template die-cast from some despotic imperative but by moving to avoid lexical sag, associated in this case with the didactic stance of a rough-grained sensibility, even if that happens to be put on. Because Purdy does not do this we sense the very sentimentality that Bowering says has been defused instead of the spry dactylity of the line, the linguistic virtuosity that helps ensure a poem's authority and truth. Technique, as Ezra Pound correctly said, is the real test of a poet's sincerity.

What Purdy and the swelling Tribe of Al have failed to take into consideration is that poetry lives in language, not in list, incident or narrative effect – which is to say, in language that is structured, alert, robust, patterned and mettlesome, language that does not simply evaporate with the reading, leaving only the subject behind. Language *is* the subject as much as the subject is itself. The tendency to write a distinctively plebeian verse is little more than an evasion of the poet's hereditary sanction, especially today as poetry grows more and more debased from an art and a calling, a pact with the tradition and a covenant with the reader, into an extensive chat with one's immediate peers or a solipsistic communing with the self.[2] Although in the case of Al Purdy, the work is rarely solipsistic; it is mainly chat with just a hint of self-communing to leaven it marginally for those who require a semblance of complexity.

The current assumption is that Purdy made it OK for us to sound like ourselves (which meant in part sounding like Purdy), but it is an unreflected assumption that begs several questions. Should we not, first, determine whether we really *do* or should even *want* to sound the way Purdy does, practising a form of mental elocution that mangles the fine syllabic discriminations required of true poetic cultivation?[3] The 'theory' on which Purdy-type poetry is built is very much like that propounded by Rameau's nephew in Diderot's great ironic farce – 'we call out, invoke, clamour, groan, weep, and laugh openly. No more witticisms, epigrams, neat thoughts – they are too unlike nature.' The result, as it should go without saying, is bathos. Second, there is obviously more than one way to sound like ourselves, living as we do in a country of plural identities still in process of formation. The dialect of Al Purdy does not exhaust our linguistic potentialities and the alternative is not

STANDARD AVERAGE CANADIAN

necessarily to sound foreign, European or derivative. And third, the best way to sound like ourselves – whatever this may ultimately mean – is to sound like ourself. But a self must be made, shaped and rendered *distinctive* not only in the moral and psychological dimensions but in the medium of language as well. Were not utterly dissimilar poets like E. J. Pratt and Leonard Cohen distinctively 'Canadian' voices before Purdy ever came demonstrably on the scene? Was not Peter Van Toorn already a *language in himself* at the time when Purdy's influence was beginning to make itself most powerfully felt? And how much more 'Canadian' can one get than Charles Bruce who, in a book like *The Mulgrave Road*, among the finest works in the treasury, gives us a poetry whose considerable technical aplomb consorts seamlessly with the language of his time and place, rendering it entirely individual?

The fact is: Purdy really made it ok for us *to sound like everyone else* and to set about, not working the language toward the cut of originality where it breaks away from the standardizing hybrid, but allowing it to sink into a kind of deflationary lingua franca, the language of mere ecphrasis. It is tempting for Purdy advocates to compare him with poets like Wordsworth (which, as I suggested, would be totally inapt) or Robbie Burns, both inordinately prolific and supposedly inspired by humble concerns knitting them to the vicissitudes and experiences of common life. At times, admittedly, a good deal of Purdy's work does tend to sound like a Canuck rendition of 'Tam o' Shanter', in which gender high jinks occur, the tavern remains a privileged venue and the place beneath the kitchen table functions occasionally as a small utopia with kids sitting in the beer crock and the grapes conferring among themselves. But although Purdy may continue to

issue proclamations to the world
and drunken manifestoes made of poem-dust and eon-mist
that say the way things ought to be
and how the drab grey rules and regs of kings and pricks
                    and man's mortality
    Stop
        short … ,

the question of talent and verbal brio would still remain to be addressed, as Purdy himself seems to recognize, no doubt facetiously, in 'On Realizing He Has Written Some Bad Poems', where he determines to

> walk among the hills chanting
> and celebrate my own failure
> transformed to something else.

In this regard, Purdy reminds me most of England's John Taylor, the Water Poet (1580–1653), popular, gregarious, and as John Aubrey wrote, 'facetious and diverting company; and for stories and lively telling of them, few could outdo him.' Earning his living as a Thames ferryman and later as bottleman at the Tower of London, he drank copiously, travelled energetically up and down the country (once sailing in a paper boat), represented the watermen in petitions to the king and was generally regarded as a spokesman for the common people. And he documented practically every episode and encounter in his life in verses so numerous that the collection, rivalling Purdy's, rises as perhaps one of the more formidable Monadnocks in the history of English poetry. In his own words,

> These Bookes in number sixty three are heere,
> Bound in one Volume, scattred here and there,
> They stand not thus in order in the booke;
> But any man may finde them, that will looke.

And if one looks long and hard enough, one will find in his first printed work, *The Sculler* (1612), an epigraph that, on the whole, will do equally well for Purdy's voluminous and laic achievement:

> Good gentle Reader, if I doe transgress,
> I know you know, that I did ne're professe,
> Vuntill this time in Print to be a Poet:
> And now to exercise my wits I show it.
> View but the intrals of this little booke,
> And thou wilt say that I some paines haue tooke:
> Paines mixed with pleasure, pleasure ioyn'd with pain
> Produc'd this issue of my laboring braine.

But there is an important difference between Taylor and Purdy, apart from those obvious and inescapable features that pertain to the linguistic apparatus associated with the times. Taylor was never taken quite seriously by his contemporaries, who appreciated his flair and bonhomie while tolerating the poetry as an expression of his eccentricity, but Purdy has been beatified as both a late, secular Franciscan and an exalted poet, the issue of whose labouring braine is an expression of the national temper and ethos. Thus Sam Solecki has courted absurdity by boosting Purdy to the top of the poet heap, comparing him in his *The Last Canadian Poet* to William Butler Yeats, thereby causing irreparable damage to the literary afterlife of his chosen laureate. This should tell us something about comparative levels of literary sophistication in seventeenth-century England and twentieth-century Canada, which appear to be almost incommutable and not to the advantage of the latter.

*  *  *

However we may respond to his work and example, there is no doubt that Purdy was a commanding figure on the Canadian poetry scene and that the effect of his poetry was central in the development of many of his younger peers and colleagues. From the early seventies on, owing to Purdy's gathering influence, Canadian poetry began to sound and look increasingly generic, as if, despite whatever differences in specific content might be found in the work of individual poets, the writing were being done by consortium. There seemed to be something like Standard Average Canadian busy at work, homogenizing the idiolect, smearing out the diction of idiosyncrasy into a dreary equivalence with most everything else that was being written at the time. And the language, as well as the attitude we tended to adopt toward the appropriate subject matter for poetry, was on the whole Purdy's, the epitome of Standard Average Canadian.

s a c as a poetic dialect was (and is) a prosy sort of medium, much susceptible to narrative pathos and weirdly reproducing in spades the palaverous superfluities that supposedly went out with the Edwardians. The poetry that Purdy gave us, it is true, embedded all the right Canadian gestures, the apotheosis of eh, but seemed ultimately better suited, given its stanchlessness and redundance, to the habits of a campfire raconteur or a drinking buddy in his cups than to the methods and linguistic comportment of a literary maker and shaper. Moreover, Purdy was unusually prone to ruining even a promising piece with the intrusion of a rather coarse and obstreperous jokiness ('Thank God I'm Normal'; 'On Being a Love-Object (*I Object*)') and voice-over expository comment ('Lament for the Dorsets'; 'At the Quinte Hotel'; – from a recurring line of which latter the N F B film on Purdy gets its title, *A Sensitive Man*). Some of the work is successful in tone and diction, as for example 'The Country North of Belleville', possibly his finest poem, where the speaker, pondering a return to his roots, concludes

> But it's been a long time since
> and we must enquire the way
> of strangers –

But these are not moments that happen often and as Purdy himself writes in 'The Beavers of Renfrew' (another all-too-rare instance), 'Every failure has flashes of genius.' In any event, it was, with a couple of exceptions, 'free verse' at its most licentious and unabashed, justifying its habitual windiness by affecting a resonant simplicity that betokened a mystical union of the contingent with the absolute.

Such was Dennis Lee's major point in the Afterword to the 1986 Collected Purdy, where he attempts to elevate what sounds like homespun cant into a numinous bond with the transcendent. Lee went on to argue that these so-called transcendent moments 'don't seem willed by the poet; they seem sponsored by being,' thus revealing a hidden, spiritual meaning in unprepossessing material. This dynamic may have worked in medieval poetry where it was called 'anagogy' but in most contemporary verse it implies dimensions of meaning that are not really there or have to be put there by partisan or impressionable readers. Goofy as the claim may now appear (the same claim Heidegger staked for the poetry of Hölderlin, where it made somewhat more sense), it changed the nature of our writing and our thinking about poetry in this country decisively.

Perhaps we would have been better off had we been able to go back and attend Jorge Luis Borges's graduate class at Columbia in the mid-seventies. Borges said to his students: 'You have to be more skilful technically to attempt free verse than to attempt what you may think of as being old-fashioned. Of course, if you happen to be Walt Whitman, you'll have the inner strength, or inner urge, that makes you capable and worthy of free verse, but this doesn't happen to many of us. My advice to young poets is to begin with the classical forms of verse and only after that, become revolutionary. [Contemporary poems] often seem to me quite meaningless ... I get the impression that the whole thing has been done in a haphazard way ... What I'm saying is that, in the long run, to break the rules, you must know *about* the rules.' But Standard Average Canadian, the language that Purdy taught us to speak, is a language without rules or precedent in the Borgian sense, the language of the public confessional that pretends to traffic with the ordinary as a pretext for the ineffable, unleashing moments of ostensibly pure incandescence and in this way legitimizing inanity. And, to recapitulate, doing so in language as undistinguished in its general tenor as it is indistinguishable in its particular embodiments.

An illustration. In some of the (dissenting) talks on Canadian poetry I give on the lecture circuit, I occasionally play a mischievous parlour game with my audience. I prepare two sets of miscellaneous poems by different hands but without attribution. The first set consists of anywhere from four to six pieces from contemporary poets *a mari usque ad mare* and the second comprises an equal number drawn from a segment of the anglophone community in Montreal, a city zoned for poetry. (A controlled segment, I should specify, since Montreal is by no means exempt from the aesthetic version of Gresham's Law.) I do not indicate the provenance of the two selections. Then I ask my audience to identify which set might be the work of a single poet and which the product of different authors. Almost invariably, the answer comes back: the Montreal batch represents the work of as many poets as there are poems but the Canada-wide anthology is the product of a single author, or a single author at different stages in his or her development. The experiment is chastening. Similarly, Carmine Starnino, writing in *Books in Canada* for December 2001, carefully examines swatches from the work of five canonical Canadian poets from Toronto and the West, concluding most convincingly: 'Five poets – five of our "best" – and only one voice among them.' Standard Average Canadian is very much the collective idiom most of the poets in this country unconsciously employ, so that the material seems to furnish an exemplary instance of the Dawkins-Blackmore replicating meme machine at work. No surprise here, since the relationship between the great majority of Canadian poets is deplorably self-referential and mutually derivative. So much for our vaunted regional differences and our creative uniqueness as practitioners of the craft.

It is true that a stethoscopic ear can detect differences and even assign identities – anyone steeped in the poetry scene over most of a lifetime will naturally acquire the facility to discriminate between (and not only against) the various poets who throng the lectern. It is also true that certain idiolects, tics and stylistic mannerisms may occasionally appear to distinguish one poet from another quite decisively, but even here – where, say, Robert Kroetsch and bill bissett go their separate lexical ways – an underlying similarity can be discerned. These poets tend to share the same anorexic diction, the same thematic frivolity and the same lack of real metaphoric power that unites them with the majority of their congeners and immediate precursors. (I have yet to meet anyone who can actually recite a single passage out of bissett – the affectation of phonetic spelling does not ensure staying power – or out of Kroetsch, whose interminable field notes bludgeon the mind by repetition into a state of insensibility.)

There is little doubt that this poetry reflects a by now typical aspiration toward the energetic laziness that followed in the wake of another deleterious influence, Northrop Frye's definitive preference, in books such as *The Bush Garden*, for a descriptive rather than evaluative criticism. The poetry of a young nation should be encouraged, he felt, and if one could not praise then one should at least refrain from censure. The result was a free-for-all of famished and imitative talents, not so much cultivators of the language as bushed gardeners. Differences exist, as conceded, between the various poets scooped up by the cowcatcher of my title, but the main point is that they are very much alike in being poor custodians of the language. And more often than not they do tend to sound eerily the same as purveyors of commonplace diction, one poem pretty well like another except for grilles, badges, cladding and minor trim. Our only hope is that Martin Amis is right when he argues in *The War against Cliché* that over the long haul, literature, like chemistry or Ancient Greek, 'will resist levelling and

STANDARD AVERAGE CANADIAN

revert to hierarchy'. But it will be a very long haul indeed. Purdy is now dead but the poetry he sponsored and underwrote is flourishing around the country like a rampant second-growth forest. And although I regret his passing, I regret his legacy even more. For as we have been told by an unimpeachable authority, light dies before the uncreating word. Over the last generation or so, following Purdy's cheerful and inchoate pied piping, we have been led into the abyss of trivial posturing, linguistic herniation and inconsiderable commentary called contemporary Canadian poetry, a poetry of leafmould, jackpine, aching subtleties and compensating sixpacks that yields at most a highly suspicious authenticity. The super-accessible strips of nearly raw experience found in Purdy's work (and in that of his disciples) are differentially readable, but not readable as *poetry*, as shaped and lovely utterance that is linguistically charged, metaphorically vital, internally structured and inherently memorable. One of Purdy's last poems, 'Say the Names', in the concluding section of the recent Collected, *Beyond Remembering*, typically requires only a map of Canada, a tolerance for the ready-made exotic and a penchant for list-making to get itself written. (The painful joke at the end of the citation is vintage Purdy.)

> Tulameen Tulameen …
> not Brighton Windsor Trenton
> but names that ride the wind
> Spillimacheen Nahami
> Kleena Kleene and Horsefly
> Illecillewaet Whachamacallit …

This is the sort of discourse that purports to be the poetry of the people. But glorying in its hypothetical anti-colonial mandate and almost relishing what Elizabeth Barrett Browning called 'the pale spectrum of the salt' beneath which the proletarian hero sits, it has become the very antithesis of the art form itself: a loose, flaccid, strolling and inventorizing variety of *written speech*. Poetry, however, is writing, not invoicing and assuredly not talking, regardless of whether the 'talking' is left to flounder on the page or laboriously revised in draft. 'Talking with Big Fanny / at Agassiz in 1963 sitting / on an old blue mattress cover / and she with her shoes off talking / and talking of Judas-Lebedoff

/ plotting against them at Wynndel' just doesn't cut it as poetry. For one of the signal tests of good poetry is its memorizability in the sense that truly good poems will often tend to *memorize themselves*. So do jingles, it might be objected, but the real point is that something as complex and involuted and even relatively lengthy as, for example, Arnold's 'Dover Beach' (or serious chunks of it), which might be expected to resist the faculty of quasi-immediate retention, practically inscribes itself on the prepared mind, whereas much shorter and less intricate poems manifestly do not. That such a thing can happen calls for explanation. And it should fairly qualify as one of the reasonable tests of fine poetry at least to the same extent as Frost's and Dickinson's famous somasthetic registrations. In any case, the point remains that we do not memorize talking (or catalogues or the public unbosomings of everyman) unless given to involuntary spasms of anamnesis, which is a pathology.

The problem, then, is that apart from a few saving exceptions we tend to commend a laic or sanscullotic verse smug in its undistinguished diction and trivial infatuations, features our literati apparently regard as a criteria of poetic virtuosity. Because we all use words, it is not surprising, as Martin Amis contends, that the literary discipline 'has rolled over for democratization', the victim of what Allan Bloom earlier called, in *Giants and Dwarfs*, 'radical egalitarianism' and 'democratic sycophancy'. In this view, we might say that Purdy is venerated because he is us and we are him and we are all equal before the word. As Bloom caustically put it, 'Every man must be understood to be creative, no matter how much the standards of art and taste have to be debauched in order to do so.' While the democratic impulse is to be cherished in the political realm, in literature it is the kiss of death: the equality of poets before the Muse like the equality of words milling on the page can lead only to the banalization of the craft. This condition is especially aggravated in Canada with its endemic insecurity and lack of any real tradition of aesthetic selectivity, which may partially explain why our poetry languishes on the borders of a barely tolerated and largely unread respectability. The irony is that the 'common reader' demands more of poetry than the unshaped transcripts and lookalike language served up by our literary populists. A poem should have the character of *singularity*, like a Ken Babstock 'Thingymajig', which is 'something they only made one / of, an imagined gadget', instructing us in the difficult art of 'valuing the devalued', as he writes in his thingymajig-packed *Days into Flatspin*.

To slice this at a different angle. What is missing in the language that Purdy, the *lar familiaris* of Canadian poetry and the incarnation of the phatic interval, taught us to speak – or write – is what Seamus Heaney in *Electric Light* calls an 'inner restitution', that is,

> … a purchase come by
> By pacing it in words that make you feel
> You've found your feet in what 'surefooted' means
> And in the ground of your own understanding.

It is precisely this inner restitution founded in language that is 'Sandy, glarry, mossy, heavy, cold' – in words as dense, thick, resilient and somatic as actual soil itself and not in a merely loose-lipped anecdotal sludge – that we need to pursue if we are to justify our practice and, for that matter, our very existence as poets. The pidgin of the humdrum encroaches like a toxic plume. But poetry lives in the power of the phrase, and although in any given poem some lines will clearly be more conspicuous and memorable than others, the good poet manages to infuse a sense of linear authority throughout in the way that a provident housewife butters bread, so that even where it is not thickly spread there is everywhere a little and no place without.

'Poetry,' said Gaston Bachelard, 'is one of the destinies of speech,' but a verbal destiny is not an undifferentiated stream of verbal events. Nor as I have argued do we commit speech to memory or recite it by heart as part of our linguistic, intellectual and cultural patrimony, as we do, for example, passages, often extensive, from Gray or Browning or Yeats or Frost or Larkin or Wilbur or Layton. The paradox is expressive. Circulating our dirges and panegyrics now that Purdy is no longer with us, clinging diligently to a consensus that feels more like unmixed adulation than sober appraisal, we all remember the man but few of us can recite the poetry. And despite sundry superficial differences, as poets we have come to resemble nothing so much as Francis Ponge's trees which think 'they can say everything, cover the entire world with assorted verbiage [but] say only "trees."' The prognosis is not good. As time goes on, exempting only a few anomalies, we sound increasingly like one another as we speak our Standard Average Canadian unmemorably into our poetry while magnifying the poet who liberated us into sameness – the poet who, with our earnest collaboration, helped us to establish not our identity but our identicalness.

———

1. Milton's famous 'darkness visible', borrowed by Golding for the title of a novel, can no longer be used in any of its permutations. A once original image is now a cliché, whether one is aware of its source or not, and sounds distressingly facile. Nor in the immediate context can one consistently argue that the allusion is deliberate, the 'quasi-romantic town of Montreal' as a specification of Pandemonium, which would at the very least have added a tincture of interest to the poem.

2. The distinction I am drawing between a 'hereditary sanction' and 'plebeian verse' has been historically displaced as the rupture between closed and open forms, which in the context of my argument is quite beside the point. (It is instructive to note that what has been designated as open verse has come to resemble a closed shop.) To extrapolate from F. O. Call's 1920 book of verse, *Acanthus and Wild Grape*, I am proposing neither the one nor the other, neither the hieratic acanthus nor the sprawling wild grape, nor, like Call, both, but something like a not wholly unaffordable ice wine native to our means and climate and yet at the same time of recognized merit. We certainly have the ice, but we learned our wine-making as part of an inheritance from elsewhere, which needs to be kept alive no matter how we proceed to modify it.

3. Such discriminations are *de rigueur* even if, as J. V. Cunningham says, 'the syllabification is that of ordinary educated speech, not of careful enunciation.' Cunningham himself expects a not-too-elastic syllabic pattern in which 'verses of seven or nine syllables are best'.

# PETER VAN TOORN

PETER VAN TOORN is the most unjustly neglected poet of our time, a poet whose genius in the language may well be unparalleled among his contemporaries. His *Mountain Tea*, which appeared in 1984 – he has published nothing since – is one of those books to which the epithet *sui generis* needs to be applied, for it can be compared to nothing else but what is similarly incomparable, that is, books without precedent or sequel, too individual, too much themselves, to beget succession (like Smart's *Jubilate Agno*, for example) yet seeding the imagination with possibility and a sense of lexical euphoria and thus propagating indirectly. In Canada I think of A. M. Klein's *The Rocking Chair and Other Poems*, James Reaney's *A Suit of Nettles*, Leonard Cohen's *The Spice-Box of Earth*, Michael Harris's *Grace* and Eric Ormsby's *Araby* as the only poetic productions that are, to put it paradoxically, equally unique – books that live wholly in their language and their mythos and cannot be separated from them. But *Mountain Tea* is a towering poetic range that we have unaccountably forgotten is there, one of the major features in our literary landscape that doesn't show up on the maps. I believe it is fair to say that Canadian poetry will not come of age until it is ready to rediscover and rehabilitate the work of Peter Van Toorn, as if in confirmation of the hope articulated in Van Toorn's signature poem, 'In Guildenstern County':

> In guildenstern county
> where there's hardly any wind
> to go by
> you can smell the poem in a thing for miles
> when wind wins.
> Wins,
> handsdown, right out of nowhere: given
> good grass out front,
> bad brush behind.

Regrettably, at the present moment, there doesn't seem to be much in the way of good grass out front (whether green or gold), as the last stanza of the poem, cancelling expectancy or perhaps merely acknowledging the reality principle, also intimates:

> In guildenstern county you can smell the lie
> for miles. In rosencrantz,
> you can buy it.

I call 'In Guildenstern County' Van Toorn's signature poem because there, in his typically feisty and lupercalian language, he assembles his principal themes in one complex structure of resonant affirmation: the vast, partially unsettled country of Canada which, despite its rawness and inhospitality to the spirit, stands as a potential analogue of the poet's imagination; the wind of freedom blowing intermittently through its people 'like a blues harp'; and the solitary traveller diving into the precambrian realm of possibility and 'surfacing in talk of: beaver, narwhal and heavy trucking.' Van Toorn's solitary traveller is a medley of apposite personae, each doing his thing: Hamlet meditating on betrayal on his voyage to England, Arnold's scholar-gypsy waiting for the light from heaven, Valentine living in the wilderness and prepared to make a virtue of necessity, knowing that home-keeping youth have ever homely wits, Jonah lost in Wawa, Ontario, running from Blake's Nobodaddy and hunting for good sex. The poem, both autobiographical and representative, balancing bitter poignancy with deprecating and at times outrageous humour, as if to mitigate dispossession, is the story of a poet on the lam searching for his Muse:

> An him go fo goofy babes,
> buff jobs,
> strappin' straw saunabone blondies …
> Watch'm sometime,
> glubby for 'em.
> Watch'm pack a tan & buick smile.

> Alpha, beta, betcha dollar
> balls that broad in his Nehru collar.

And indeed, on further reflection, almost *any* poem in the collection gives evidence of a superb talent at the height of its powers. *Mountain Tea* is the work of what we might call a *natural* poet, at one with the concrete world around him, and yet at the same time the most rigorous of verbal disciplinarians, one who still remembers how to gaffle a line. Van Toorn is the poet of the hundredth draft, crafting and polishing incessantly to create his proprietary effect of lines drumming across and down the page in an impetuous syllabic race to the temporary haven of closure, like his Mountain Fox 'with a peppering of paws on the crust' of the snow-stiff grass. What we get is a poetry that is both impeccable and footloose, absolutely precise in its diction and metrics but explosive in its impact. In fact, he reminds me of his own Mountain Maple, who is 'a cross between man and grass, and / grow[s] in the thought of him from the ground up.' And also of his shimmery Dragonfly, 'much more truly quotable, / more strictly independent and severe,' than practically any other poet in the country.

Another (and yet related) aspect of Van Toorn's performance, which makes him something of an anomaly in the context of Canadian verse, is the almost complete absence of the personal pronoun. The confessional streak so dear to his fellows and one of the chief hallmarks of our national poetry is scarcely to be found anywhere in his work. Van Toorn works by indirection, like a wizard shopping in Diagon Alley. Revelations of self are anathema to him as if he knew that the anecdotal infatuation and its compulsion to render private experience public were a sign either of nonage or dotage. Rather he has made an investment of self in the very language he deploys so that, even though he stays clear of mere avowal and revelation, it is virtually impossible not to recognize a Van Toorn 'product' should you come across it on the bookshelf and turn the pages absent-mindedly. Before you know it you are larruped into awareness by a poem – if I may cite – that just jeeps up, 500 turkeys on each hubcap for traction. You awaken to a poetry that takes constant issue with the bland pro-formas of standard lexical exchange and puts the devil in the bar code. In short, you have made the acquaintance of Peter Van Toorn, a.k.a. Bojo Harang, coming through the sticky pines, all blugy'n bulgy, riggin dat slapstuff, who gives us poems that are full of poetry, not of the poet.

In a way, Van Toorn, who was born in Holland, reminds me of his contemporary and approximate landsman, the Flemish painter Leo Copers, whose work is a unified congeries of unexpected materials collected with a pica-like appetite from the entire natural and artifactual creation. See for example Coper's notable 1997 *Untitled* installation which consists of six vases, red wine, gold rope and thread, and a used boning knife, or his 1991 *Untitled* redoubte print made from a pair of gloves, human blood, cardboard, fibreglass, velvet and copperleaf. Similarly, Van Toorn is an architectonic magpie gathering his materials from everywhere and arranging them in the best, most startling and yet wholly appropriate order, every word, phrase and stanza shack on and flemished down unerringly.

The republication of *Mountain Tea*, corrected and revised, almost twenty years after it was allowed to fall into oblivion, is an important event in the cultural life of our country. As I suggested above, it is the reader more than the poet who is the beneficiary of the occasion. To apply the political lingo of the province of Quebec, where Van Toorn has lived all his adult life, our 'poetic nation' will not achieve its independence as a viable and sovereign entity until it satisfies a number of winning conditions, of which one of the most salient is the belated recognition of the bare handful of truly distinguished poets it has improbably nourished. Of these, Peter Van Toorn is one of the most eminent.

# REFLECTIONS ON THE
# LAUREATESHIP

Poets with laureates, sinecures of creative writing, and other epaulets of offi-
cial verse culture must resign their commissions, withholding their services
until poetry matters.

— Michael Corbin, *Baltimore City Paper*

> Shall we go round the mulberry bush, or shall
> We gather at the river, or shall we
> Appoint a Poet Laureate this fall,
> Or shall we have another cup of tea?
>
> — Frank Scott, *The Canadian Authors Meet*

THE ISSUE OF WHETHER OR NOT to establish a parliamentary poet
laureate in this country has been much debated of late by poets and par-
liamentarians. The fact that the measure has now been adopted and a
laureate chosen has by no means stilled the controversy but continues to
incite barbed exchanges among a specialized community of belligerents.
Those who favour the laureateship claim that it is an expression of the
national will toward a collective identity and point out that mature
democracies like the U.K. and the U.S. have long cherished the institu-
tion. Opponents view the laureateship as a superfluous and unaf-
fordable luxury, if not as a safehouse for incompetents.

Some poets like to invoke 'the people' whose passionate democratic
yearnings should be given formal embodiment in the laureateship,
which they see as a bastion and condition of freedom. Others have
observed that great or very good poets seldom receive (or accept) such
posts, which naturally prize all that is conventional and inoffensive.
Although there are some instances to the contrary (e.g., Ted Hughes in
the U.K. and Richard Wilbur in the U.S., even if they too were
compromised), the negative view tends to be borne out by the

commonplace travesty of too many laureates over the course of their tenure churning out drivel on demand to mark this or that public occasion. As critic A. N. Wilson writes in the *Guardian* (February 18, 2002), 'this is just journalism set to verse. The whole concept of the poet laureate is completely ridiculous ... And the forced subjects are bound to make the poetry worse.' Thus Andrew Motion in England now belies his surname and the current American holder of the office (as of this writing), Billy Collins, will probably find a heretofore intriguing populist muse sadly frumpified by his appointment. (His elegy for the victims of 9-11, 'The Names', is a case in point: a noble sentiment, to be sure, but a flatlined poem replete with recycled clichés and shopworn images and devices, which, *as a poem*, does little honour to his subject.)[1] As for the previous incumbent, Stanley Kunitz at the age of ninety-five was just as potent as any of his more youthful and presumably more vigorous peers – the obligations of the job guarantee the dreariness and banality for which the poet need no longer strive. The first Canadian appointee is George Bowering, a poet of such modest talents that he may well be immune to the noxious effects of the laureateship. The damage has already been done, fifty books' worth of it.

Clearly, it is hard to avoid a sort of creeping ideological servility as well as a profaning of aesthetic standards once one has agreed to represent the status quo. For the laureate would have no sanction to censure and reprove, neither to object to national policy nor reproach public mores as poets have always felt free to do. Further, the need to bat out odes and commemorations on demand is a surefire recipe for poetic disaster. As American poet and critic William Logan reminds us, 'poets suffer when they speak not for themselves but for a country. Taste is the enemy of patriotic sentiment – we would not have to appoint a poet laureate otherwise.' Good poetry cannot often be produced on spec or on commission any more than oysters secrete pearls because jewelers want them to. Even Inaugural poems tend to be distressingly bad (Frost's was an exception), as witness Maya Angelou's 'On The Pulse Of Morning', read on 20 January 1993, which should have embarrassed Bill Clinton far more than Monica Lewinsky's subsequent oral performances. The fact that Angelou has recently sold her 'talents' to the Hallmark greeting card company should come as no surprise. Indeed, we can now all look forward to the impending *Maya Angelou Life Mosaic Collection* and a new line of products including verse-inscribed mugs, bookends, pillows, wall hangings and journal booklets as a likely prelude to a future laureateship.[2]

As far as Canada is concerned, there are simply not enough good poets in the country to be showcased as laureates (in the original sense of the term) or to redeem the actual laureateship from the mediocrity it both expects and fosters. Of course, we have no shortage of aspiring bards – the number of poets per capita is probably higher in Canada than in any other country, including Ireland. But the trouble is that most of them are poets whose principal relation to poetry is histrionically mimetic, as if in imitation of the Wayne Johnston alcoholic in *The Colony of Unrequited Dreams* who, when sober, 'would wander around the house as though in imitation of sobriety, as if not entirely sure what it was that sober people did.' Only, in this circumstance our poets do not seem to be entirely sure what it is that word-intoxicated people are supposed to do.

What the 'poetic' advocates of the laureateship are really talking about is not excellence and creative vigour but privilege and preferment. When it was asserted by one of our much-published poets that the laureate should be appointed 'by a jury of his or her peers', we should have smelled the rat immediately. Even if a different method of selection has been installed – a committee of poets, parliamentarians and Canada Council bureaucrats acting at different stages in the process of nomination and choice – we can rest assured that the results do not inspire confidence, let alone poetry. We would have been far better advised to have thought seriously on a passage from a letter of Thomas Gray where the poet assures his correspondent: 'if any great man would say to me "I make you rat-catcher to his Majesty, with a salary of 300 pounds a year and two butts of the best Malaga ..." I cannot say I should jump at it, nay, if they would drop the very name of the office, and call me Sinecure to the King's Majesty, I should still feel a little awkward, and think everybody I saw smelt a rat about me.'

But there is another reason apart from the inward corruption of motive which vitiates so much of the poetry being mass-produced around us, as is evident to anyone who takes the time to scan the scene and reflect unsentimentally. Our poets are on the whole so earnest and proactive in pursuing their various *nonpoetic* goals they resemble the

Energizer Bunny on a rampage. Having become ™ poets, they give too much of their vitality to the *business* of poetry: the organization of rotas, granting structures, festivals, awards, unions, trusteeships, writing spas, frequent reading junkets, manifesto journals, conference calls, poetry textbooks and anthologies aimed at the school market, and the construction of editorial and *de facto* power centres. Scottish writer William McIlvanney recalls attending a meeting of the League of Canadian Poets in Vancouver some years ago, which, he reports, resembled 'a convention of salespeople whose only product was themselves'. The poets 'talked enough about money to be chartered accountants'. But the League is far more than a mere talking shop. It is an emporium where the thin men of Haddam dream of snaring golden birds and the bawds of euphony cry out sharply.

It is therefore no wonder that very little energy or dedication is left over for the painstaking writing of good poems, which arise only from an imagination that is primed, driven, self-trained, independent, in love with language and radically unsparing if not draconian in the criteria it habitually invokes to judge its efforts by. This is not to say that our poets are not prolific, which they are to a fault, but that is precisely the point: *a decent poem takes time.* And that is why far too many of the poems written by the overwhelming majority of our poets read as if they had been phoned in, read like a betrayal of the original impetus and initiative that fires the poetic imagination, even when, as so often happens here, the subject seems morally lofty or socially responsible. Richard Sanger is spot on when he maintains in an article in the *Globe and Mail* for December 12, 1990, that most of these efforts remain 'suspect since they tend to confuse the justice of certain social causes with the advancement of the poet's own career.' In any event, for all its apparent hustle and concern, Canadian poetry needs to be medevaced to Parnassus pronto if it is to have any chance of recovery.

The point is, of course, that all the frantic activity uniting our poets is really quite meretricious, ironically masking a sort of mortuary stillness, a torpidness of vision and discipline making itself felt in the drab and insipid quality of the work itself. They remind me – most of them – of Chaucer's Man at Law: 'Nowher so bisy a man as he ther nas / And yet he seemed bisier than he was.' As for the laureates to be selected every second year from the vast pool of potential claimants, considering the round of social obligations that necessarily come with the appointment, they will, I'm afraid, furnish the sorry theatrics of titivating parvenus of whom it might be said that the sartorial deputizes for the intellectual and mere junket-bustle serves to compensate for lack of genuine flair and substance. Like Richard Cory, they will glitter when they walk, but only when they walk.

We are fortunate, it should be said, in being blessed with a sparse modicum of exceptional and *singular* poets in our midst who labour reliably at the jobsite – our poets aureate who are so seldom fêted or featured. But there are not enough of these sons and daughters of Los to choose from in order to sustain the kind of institution the laureateship is supposed to be and there is no guarantee that they would be elected to the office, let alone that they would wish to be. A far more likely scenario is that the laureateship will continue to be filled by the lek of second-raters and time-servers, the purveyors of pack poetry, whose serial candidacies must be seen as a virtual certainty. The chances of their raising the level of debate in the Commons – one of the stated aims of the appointment – must be less than nil, not only because our parliamentarians are for the most part unteachable nonentities for whom Churchill is half the name of a small northern community but because our poets are equally strangers to the noble art of rhetorical tournure. Are our interests really to be served by having, say, a Bowering, followed by a Borson, a Brand, a Blodgett, a Bök, a Clarke, a Crozier or a Kroetsch representing the collective spirit of the people? What does this say about the people? The names of Margaret Atwood, Leonard Cohen and Stompin' Tom Connors were also floated by one of the participants in the Senate proceedings. But according to Alliance M P Deborah Grey, Atwood would have been considered inappropriate – not, be it said, for her pedestrian poetry but for her opposition to the free trade agreement! So much for creative and intellectual liberty. Cohen, who has already turned down a Governor General's Award, is far too principled and independent a writer ever to accept such a post (and besides, he has written very little poetry over the last thirty years). As for Stompin' Tom, he is, quite simply, not a poet at all. These suggestions merely demonstrate how far from the literary world our laureate campaigners live.

On balance, I think it is fair to say that Senator Jerry Grafstein and

MP Marlene Jennings were not doing the country a favour when they undertook a parliamentary bill to endow so problematic an apparatus, one whose predominant effect is to cater to the sense of literary and political chauvinism that habitually motivates us and which is ultimately, to borrow a phrase from Davenant's *Gondibert*, only a 'monument to vanished minds.' I agree wholeheartedly with Jennings that 'poetry is important' and that it is the very 'soul of a nation', as she claimed not so long ago on CBC's *As It Happens*, but that is precisely why I have opposed the laureateship so emphatically. A nation should not disgrace itself.

We should twig instantly to the self-interested and partisan rhetoric which laureate backers have tended to mobilize in their rapt involvement with what David Barber, a poet and *Atlantic Monthly* staff editor, calls 'Po-Biz hustle and para-literary free enterprise.' The League's newsletter for February 21 (2000) enthusiastically supported Ms. Jennings' recommendation that poets lobby their MPs for support, called attention to its own role in bringing the idea 'to reality', and blared with adolescent punstership: 'Now is the time for all good literati to come to the aid of the Poetry!' Talk about special pleading! The climate of self-aggrandizement we find here must give the serious observer pause and provoke the obvious question: how cynical can one get about what is theoretically meant to operate as a poetic and cultural restorative? But then, when it comes to the cynics, there's no cure like a sinecure.

The dilemma, as I've suggested, is that a select few of our poets are too good to act as the position *actually* demands and the rest just not good enough to act as the position *ideally* requires. In the latter case, one could argue that the poet and the position *as presently constituted* deserve each other, to the discredit of us all. The salary and expense account that would accompany the presumed service would be nothing less than a waste of taxpayer's money. Even an honorarium of a few hundred pounds and a butt of sack would be overly generous. Andrew Waterman writing in the *PN Review* for September/October 1999 puts it on the money: 'All in all, the prospect of aspiring placepersons scrabbling ... for preferment to a Laureateship which is now a salaried post is grisly.'

But plainly it is not only the vigorish that impels poets to seek the laureateship. Ian Hamilton sheers very close to the truth, I suspect, when in an article on the question in the *London Review of Books* for 7 January 1999, he conjectures that 'Maybe poets want to be Laureates because they secretly fear that they've already made the most of whatever gifts they started out with. Since nobody expects a P L to be any good, why not accept the job and let *it* take the blame for your next book?'

The Canadian context is probably not so very different from the American or the British, despite the weird assumption on the part of many of our poets that absence of talent is in their case no obstacle to greatness and, as specified by The Writers' Union of Canada, provides no grounds for literary discrimination. After all, one should not be held *personally* responsible for having been born without gifts. (There *is* one characteristic difference: the debate often bogged down in the language question as the participants in the controversy haggled over whether the laureate was to write in English, French or Inuktitut.) The activating factors for most of the suitors for the post irrespective of their national stripe and cultural mindset have little to do with the writing of good poetry. And the unacknowledged effect of their election will be to ensure a flavourless conformity and to contribute to the collective cultural snooze, none of them like to the Larkin at break of day arising. (When Philip Larkin was asked in an interview whether he ever dreamed about the laureateship, he replied that he did but always woke up screaming.) Moreover, now that we have elected a laureate, we can proceed to forget about poetry even more thoroughly than we already have since perhaps the most important function of the laureateship, at any rate from the perspective of its secular lobbyists, is to appease the national conscience as well as their own for the apathy and neglect with which they receive the art. Of one thing we can be absolutely sure. The position will not be filled with poets like those Shelley depicts in *Adonais* as 'kings of thought / Who waged contention with their time's decay.'

Let us consider for a moment the original documentation itself, a transcript of the Proceedings of the Standing Committee on Social Affairs, Science and Technology for Wednesday, March 29, 2000, on the subject of Bill s-5 (later upgraded to s-10) for the appointment of a parliamentary poet laureate. This document begins with a long and confused rhapsody on the virtues of poetry by the Hon. Jerahmiel S.

Grafstein, which reads as if it had been researched and prepared by a coven of ghost writers. Segueing into an analysis of a digitally imploding civilization, it goes on to prescribe the *institution* of poetry as an sovereign antidote to social anomie, a remedy the senator or his surrogates define as, among other things, an 'alternate vice'. (Hopefully, this is a misprint for 'voice'.) Poetry is cried up as a universal panacea for almost all of the ills that bedevil our society – not including, however, poetry itself or at least that species of the art that has assumed currency among us. Nevertheless, the laureate would have a relatively easy time of it since he or she would serve with only '*minimalist* responsibilities' (italics mine). In the course of the debate, Senator Roche proposes establishing a 'photographer laureate' as well. While not disagreeing overtly, Senator Grafstein opines that the word should take precedence over the image since, if I understand him correctly, parliament is an acoustic phenomenon, and besides 'It would be nice having a poet laureate around.' National Librarian Roch Carrier, a well-known writer himself, gives further support to the bill by asserting that Canada 'has hundreds of poets ... that are writing good poetry', that is to say, there would seem to be more poets writing good poetry in Canada than there are in the entire world, paradoxically including Canada. Unless Mr Carrier has discovered a hitherto unsuspected property of infinite sets, namely that they can be exceeded by their subsets, it appears that his math may be as exaggerated and improbable as his capacity for critical appraisal.

Mr Carrier then proceeds to tout the benefits of the Canadian Poetry Archive Internet site that will shortly feature the work of one hundred early Canadian poets. What is even worse, 'some of these poems will be recorded so that those who are visually impaired will be able to hear the poetry,' as if these people were not already sufficiently afflicted. The spectacle of a constituency of blind poetry lovers soliciting help from sighted friends and relatives merely to access this archive would be laughable were it not so discouraging. (Whatever happened to the Carrier who once said in a newspaper interview that 'Humour is an exercise of the soul'?) Roger Nash, a professor at Laurentian University and a past president of the League of Canadian Poets who first brought up the notion of the laureateship, weighs in next with the suggestion that the laureate should also possess 'public relations skills' to supplement his or her quasi-ambassadorial duties, cheerfully skipping over the fact that some of the most celebrated poets of the modern era were veritable frankenfish: terminal drunks, suicide-prone depressives, spouse beaters, stony recluses, professional troublemakers, reactionary throwbacks with a taste for autocracy and a hankering for police states, social incompetents and insufferable bores. (What would a selection committee make of someone like Tom Wolfe's not-so-far-fetched, Nobel-shortlisted, supercilious, effete, AIDS-suffering Lord Aubrey Buffing – or would that be Aubrey Lord Buffing –, son of the fitly named Duke of Bray, who comes to the astounding conclusion that reproduction is the true purpose of life?) Even more troubling from the standpoint of a public institution, an elite cohort of these poets were revolutionary firebrands who insisted on speaking their minds regardless of consequences – so much for public relations skills. Mr Nash also seems blissfully unaware that his privileging of the poets themselves in the selection process could lead only to sycophantic excesses or endemic factionalism. Finally, the chairman of the Committee, the Hon. Michael Kirby, concurs with the peer review proposal on the partial grounds of his 'having been an ex-professor myself.' One cannot help but wonder what he was before having been an ex-professor, or after for that matter.

I would suggest that this is a document eminently suited to furnishing a bit of entertainment on a cold and bleak Canadian winter evening and I would recommend its perusal to anyone in need of a little harmless distraction – although the *effects* of Bill s-10 will be by no means harmless and can only bring our cultural life to even lower levels of collective desuetude. With so inept a maniple of standard bearers, one may perhaps legitimately inquire why these proceedings were not staged on *This Hour Has 22 Minutes* or *Royal Canadian Air Farce* rather than in the august chambers of the Senate. On second thought, the distinction may be moot. Or if one were susceptible to conspiracy theories, one might be excused for believing that our pundits and power-brokers are trying to dismantle the nation's poetry from the top, as owner Jeffrey Loria did with the Montreal Expos baseball team. Only, in this case, our new-found Loriats will be actively colluding in the process.

Be that as it may, I suspect that now it has become a reality, the entire project will be greeted with massive public indifference – though the trickle-down effect cannot be discounted. Robert Fulford writing in the

*National Post* (December 15, 2001) handles the issue with gentle tact, regarding it as unlikely that a national bard who excites 'the affections of the people … will emerge through the laureate system', but qualifies his scepticism by piously suggesting 'miracles can happen'.

The real miracle is that our poets continue to profit at the national expense through the chaperoning agency of guilds, granting bodies and standing committees, which seem to proliferate annually and whose unaccountable largesse is sometimes quite staggering. Such considerations ought to have given us ample reason for slow and prudent deliberation – for a kind of publishing of banns – before proceeding to solemnize the marriage of mediocrity and nepotism whose offspring will pester us for generations to come.

---

1. Collins is tapping into our emotions as well as our sentimentality, which effectively prevents us from judging the poem on its own merits, as if this would constitute an act of disrespect to the dead or a failure of patriotism. The poem is, so to speak, radiant with our own prior disposition. Galway Kinnell's 'When the Towers Fell' is a far worthier performance.

2. An example of the kind of crockery couplet we can expect from Angelou may be found on the Internet at the Guardian Unlimited Books site, where we read *inter alia:* 'Life is a glorious banquet, / a limitless and delicious buffet', lines which no doubt have an increasingly autobiographical application.

# ARDOUR ILLUMINATES

ardor
illuminating with its terrifying currency
now no mere glimpse, no porthole vista
but, down on down, the uninhabitable sorrow.
– Amy Clampitt, *The Kingfisher*

THE MEASURE OF A STRONG BOOK of poems – to apply Brooks
Hansen's useful distinction – lies in the proportion of effigy to totem, of
things resembling something else to things looking like what they are
supposed to look like. In *Questions for Ecclesiastes,* Tennessee poet Mark
Jarman has given us a book of poems that is engagingly and memorably
totemic, a volume with a modicum of effigies – far less than what most
practitioners of the art consider acceptable – and a staunch majority of
totems that jostle for memory space. These are poems that are not
merely exercises in self-expression but the *real thing:* poems by which we
may try to locate ourselves in the tracklessness of contemporary life.

   The book is divided into five sections, the first two and last two treat-
ing of domestic affairs and everyday experiences set in a quasi-theolog-
ical context that renders them poignant and suggestive. The central
section of twenty 'unholy sonnets' serves as the pivot on which the
events of daily existence turn and acquire coherence. It is without doubt
this cynosure suite which helps to make the book one of those memo-
rable collections that offer to become a part of that daily existence. The
whole is in many ways a compelling achievement, an arresting mix of
the ordinary and extraordinary, of moments in the rose garden
intersecting with small lifetimes of rank ailanthus, of everyday lines and
phrases suddenly illumined by vivid images and incantatory passages
taking the reader out of the datum, the artifactual poem on the page,
and into the empyrean of poetry itself. It is the kind of book that makes
a difference.

   In other words, to use Jarman's own phrase, these poems are

'transformed by resistance' to the drift toward temporal and spiritual entropy that characterizes the age in which we live. They are poems that give us, often when we least expect it, 'the word made ... gooseflesh.' 'Questions For Ecclesiastes', the title piece which sets the tone for the rest of the book, is a brave poem about questions that need insistently to be posed regarding the purposes of life and death, questions that, if we are honest, we know will go unanswered. God is good at keeping secrets, Jarman suggests, although as a later poem discloses, God is the secret we cannot keep.

The suite of seven meditative lyrics (if that is the right word) called *The Past From The Air* is among the most technically adroit, yet emotionally moving and seemingly *spontaneous* poems that I have read in years. Each section resurrects a moment from a family attic of heirloom memories with which every reader can empathize. For example, section 4 ('Praying') describes in impeccable *ottava rima* the ordinary act of washing dishes as a child observes his mother

> doing three things, watching a cloud pass,
> talking to God, drying a drinking glass.

But the child is not alone in his act of observation. God is there too, but

> the god to whom she is praying
> ... sees a woman asking him to read
> her mind. He pities her. He cannot read.

Only *we* can read. But we cannot intervene. Nor can we redeem except in memory and awareness the pathos and suffering of our powerlessness.

Or consider section 6 ('The Apparition'), which plies an artful allusion to Pound's celebrated Metro poem, to the phantom faces the precursor poet meets in the Hades of the Underground and to the 'wet, black bough' that ironically recalls the golden bough of Book 6 of the *Aeneid* – the latter permitting the return to the light but the former an organic and, as it were, biodegradable one-way ticket into the darkness. Yet memory and awareness are stubbornly at work in the subtle way the piece remembers the poem in which Pound remembers Virgil's description of Avernus. Poets may continue to write and cite, that is, to remain literate in the face of semantic dispersion, even though they are condemned to practise their trade in a world presided over by a divine illiteracy. And if they are good poets, to do so in the most crafty and attentive of ways which serve, rather than militate against, a deep sincerity of feeling.

The book, as noted, is so constructed as to centralize the sequence of twenty *Unholy Sonnets*, one more than the nineteen of Donne's original suite of *Holy Sonnets* (not counting the aperitive seven he sent to Magdalen Herbert). It is as if Jarman were recycling Donne into the present age by momentum and increment, setting up resonances and concentricities that thematically incorporate not only his great forerunner and model but also, I suspect, Galway Kinnell's divan of 13-liners (one less line than the sonnet, betokening incompleteness) entitled *When One Has Lived A Long Time Alone*, and, in Jarman's own fifteenth sonnet, Robert Frost's gnostic 'Design'. In this way the unholy sonnets, invigorated by allusion and context, derive a kind of surplus energy that permits them to question, reflect upon and confront the unrepresentable with a certain brio and confidence that will not be deterred by the lack of response or correspondence. The poems approach and recede from the mystery of a silent Creation – of the paradox of 'grace that fill[s] emptiness' alternating with an absence only 'the stars adore' – in (to quote Donne) 'devout fitts [that] come and go away / Like a fantastique Ague,' as if in a conflicting access of bravado and despair, assurance and agitation that constitutes the dominant tone of the whole.

For there is, it must be admitted, something flushed and mercurial, even feverish, about the whole performance, lit by striking metaphors (the nails of steepling fingers fitting tight like 'welders' masks') and flaring into sonnets of consummate brilliance (like the sixteenth, which begins 'We drove to the world's end'), yet occasionally flatlining ('and seeing is believing and being seen,' a Berkeleian bromide) or lapsing into rather slight practicums like the twelfth sonnet which merely retreads an old joke. But this is no doubt a minor quibble for it is notoriously difficult to sustain any sort of poetic excellence over a long catena of verbal, linear and formal effects, especially when the poet is confronting the great Silence. (Even Donne suffers from his inescapable *longueurs* and one cannot help but wonder whether the *Holy Sonnets* would continue to be read if the seventh, tenth and fourteenth entries did not rescue the whole from a resident excess of fustian and platitude.) Jarman is to be congratulated on his resourcefulness and skill, the adeptness that enables him to achieve the notable symbiosis of form and content that makes *Unholy Sonnets*, despite its desultory falterings, a work to be consulted, pondered and frequently reread, helping us to fill with sentient and interrogative presence the uninhabitable sorrow of God's apparent absence.

It is much easier to talk about poetry than it is to talk about God, and so I will conclude with a brief reflection on the much debated but not wholly transparent movement called the New Formalism, of which Jarman is an acknowledged spokesman and practitioner. Perhaps this capacity we see in Jarman's work to marry genuine substance with technical proficiency is what is intended by the term. For myself, when it comes to weighing the merits and demerits of the school, I fail to see what the theoretical fuss is about. Anne Stevenson, writing in a collection of essays entitled *After New Formalism*, justifiably takes exception to the 'ism', which transforms the 'movement' into another reified abstraction prone to 'misinterpretation in our present world, in which historical imagination and sensibility play so small a part'. There is more to formalism, she suggests, than rhyme and metre, or, I would add, than cathecting on any given set of rules.

It is, of course, impossible to define the root term adequately, but I would hazard the following: assuming we are successful, form is what sometimes happens when we have something both difficult and worthy of respect to work against, something that requires a structured efficiency as a countervailing agent against the defiant mutabilities of both language and our experience of the world. Form is traction. Michael Donaghy is surely right when he claims, in a not entirely favourable review of the Jarman/Mason anthology *Rebel Angels*, that the precise function of form is the 'serendipity provided by negotiation with a resistant medium, the intervention of what we used to call the muse', rather than the conscious effort to produce a 'seminar topic' that illustrates the premises of a *movement*. In Donaghy's terms, we might say that form is a way of resisting resistance, of gaining paradoxical purchase on what is at the same time frictionless and impregnable.

Further, I would suggest that the epithet 'new' is equally misleading, as it almost always is. After all, what have totemic poets like Philip Larkin, James Merrill and Richard Wilbur been doing for a generation and more if not precisely what the implicit manifesto behind the New Formalism so resonantly summons poets to attempt? The point I am trying to make with respect to Mark Jarman is not that his work is 'new' or that it exhibits a 'formalist' bent, terms I regard as mere adjectival excrescences synthetically attached to the substantive 'poetry', but that it illuminates because it is ardent in both its strong conviction and its grappling with the inherited staples of the craft. We are reading a poet who, sponsored by his illustrious predecessors, commands the technical *means* to clarify or generate *meaning*, and who has something of importance to say to all of us.

In any case, it is reassuring to know that the Muse has placed a Jarman in Tennessee and that the slovenly wilderness may one day, if Jarman's example in this book catches on and if the poet himself continues to produce work of this quality, be pruned into unaccustomed order.

# AN OPEN LETTER
# TO LORNA CROZIER

DEAR LORNA,

I am writing to suggest that it might be a good idea to go easy on contributing oracles on the writer's life to the Book Pages of our newspapers, as you recently did in the Literary Section of the Montreal *Gazette*. You should keep in mind that our country, despite all the literary agitprop, is not favoured by very many writers whose talent and verbal élan merit being heard. In fact, I strongly suspect that the sort of exposure you afford them – and yourself – may lead not to public enlightenment but to personal embarrassment. We are not so far, really, from the 'clerks' in Pope's *Dunciad* who, 'in one lazy tone / Through the long, heavy, painful page drawl on.'

Your most recent effort is, I regret to say, a veritable gumbo of clichés, self-indulgent posturings and phrases of almost surpassing innocence. You admit that poetry 'will never sell as well as the most obscure novel' or that it won't 'match the sales' of self-help books, but that nevertheless 'it ends up paying off' because of its demands, which are, presumably, equivalent to its rewards. No committed poet ever doubted the sad truism that there is no money in poetry and no serious poet ever put pen to paper with that in mind. Why even mention it? The marketing allusion betokens a banausic sensibility that has absolutely no point of contact with the genuine poetic afflatus, and the commercial metaphor only makes matters worse. Poetry did not 'pay off' for the great Paul Celan who took his own life in despair of language ever being able to 'ransom' the atrocities of our century into a kind of speakableness.

As for the apparent benefits of poetry to which you refer, namely, that it 'insists you walk through the day with rapt attention' or that, *mirabile dictu*, it enables you, 'against all the odds', to recover the evanescent past ('the father who used to throw you high in the air with his strong arms' – thankfully his arms weren't weak), well, I'm sorry to say but poetry has no monopoly on such incandescent moments. Any sentient person with a memory, clearly, will and does vividly recall 'the childhood house you once walked into'. Any alert human being with eyes will and does delight in 'the translucent antennae of a snail'. If poetry helps you to marvel at an apricot-size batrachian, I see no reason for you to deny yourself this pleasure. But I also see no reason to claim it as a special boon bestowed by the ineffable muse to which poets like yourself apparently have privileged access. As a poet knowledgeable in the tradition, you must surely recall those salient lines of Keats from *The Fall of Hyperion*:

> Who alive can say,
> 'Thou art no Poet – may'st not tell thy dreams?'
> Since every man whose soul is not a clod
> Hath visions, and would speak, if he had loved,
> And been well nurtured in his mother tongue.

Or the conclusion Milton Acorn comes to after studying the mountain for three years:

> And nothing had impressed me so much
> That the poem is not the thing ...

Most unfortunately, however, you go on to assert what many good poets have said before you, that poetry 'is the place where language is revived.' (Eliot/Mallarmé: poetry purifies the dialect of the tribe.) I say 'most unfortunately', because your examples and the style in which they are tenanted give the lie outright to your protestation. The article you published, no less than your pseudo-flashy but halting verse, sees to it only that language stumbles from the tongue to expire on the page. 'When I get a poem right,' you solemnly aver, it is 'as if a spark has leapt across a distance not crossed before.' I find this claim as typical as I do objectionable. The spark-across-the-gap image has been used so many times before that the engine now fails to start. Moreover, this supposedly incendiary achievement is not for the poet to say but for the reader or the critic. The latter will determine whether the poem sizzles or not while the poet, modestly retiring from the business of dispensing kudos for self-accomplishment, will refrain from plugging her own work. A spark plug, as it were.

But the melancholy fact is that the kind of writing I am targeting here rarely scintillates at all, and I suspect that the reason for this may have something to do with the constitutive narcissism of its 'creators'. In other words, the relaxed and flaccid quality of the writing with which I am taking issue in this letter seems to come from an *exaggeration* of one's importance as a poet or, what amounts to the same thing, the exaggeration of one's subject and place, usually a substitute for the self-regarding self and thus a device for making criticism and revision sublimely irrelevant. Alice Meynell made the point nearly a century ago in *Hearts of Controversy:* 'We resent exaggeration if we care for our English language. For exaggeration writes relaxed, and not elastic, words and verse.' So come off your high horse, Lorna; it isn't Pegasus.

You go on to mourn 'the death of our cat', clearly not the pensive Selima. You confide in your 'lover' that you want 'to understand' and 'to connect' with the larger world. Finally you conclude that you will continue to write poetry 'against all the odds'. Again, battered by this farrago of nonsense, I must object. As any real writer knows, there are no odds to write against because one does not write for that reason. Cats, lovers and odds aside, the only 'wager' is with one's own spirit. One doesn't write for money. One doesn't write from an agenda. One doesn't write to confer blessings on the inarticulate. One doesn't write because the language has commissioned one to save it. *Who do you think you are anyway?* One writes because one loves what one is doing or because one is driven. One writes because – in the words of Robert Melançon from *Exercices de Désoeuvrement,* a necessary meditation on the craft and mystery of the calling – '*Un poème n'a pas à rendre mes goûts, mes humeurs, les accidents qui sont ma substance. J'écris pour devenir plus que "moi".*' In the last analysis, one writes because one writes, come what may or may not. And one publishes only in diffidence and insecurity, dreading to impose upon the reader but hoping at the same time that the work has been conceived in love that is both *genuine and commutative*, despite the absence of any guarantee. As Thomas Lux puts it in 'An Horatian Notion',

Grow up! Give me, please, a break!
You make the thing you love because you love the thing
and you love the thing because someone else loved it
enough to make you love it.
And with that your heart like a tent peg pounded
toward the earth's core ...
And with that you go to work.

And if you do happen to redeem the language in the process, then you have my gratitude and congratulations. But lexical redemption arrives as an unintended benefit, a donation from the Muse. Let her take the credit, or at least, let someone else give it to you for the noble service you have performed.

I admit that I mount this critique from a pronounced bias and I obviously do not shun polemics, but I must reiterate that I have never been partial to poets who claim to speak for the people, as you apparently do, or who preen themselves in composing out of a populist mindset. In the greater share of these instances, I believe that the people deserve better. Certainly the people should not be subjected to the presumably good offices of their unelected advocates or – heaven forbid – legislators, Shelley notwithstanding. In any event, I encounter far richer language in the streets than I do in the tepid pages of most Canadian poetry, of which you regard yourself as an important exemplar. If I wanted to get into more trouble with my peers, I could list another three dozen 'resonant' names at the drop of a beret or a bonnet. Please note that I'm not trying to point out that the emperor has no clothes, but to suggest that there is no emperor there in the first place, dressed or otherwise.

Of course, in addition to the spread of the majoritarian muse, the larger tractarian context in which much of our poetry is now being written and discussed tends to fudge the real issue. Male poets have gone politically correct, taking care not to offend anyone, especially female poets, either in their verse or their critical overviews. Female poets, with some notable exceptions, are prone to glorying in the unearned accomplishment of gender, transforming a fact of nature into an aesthetic manifesto and a cannibalizing literary movement. The spectacle of a sorority of Widow Blackacres – Wycherley's most comic and memorable chararacter, from *The Plain Dealer*, a masculine, litigious, pettifogging, headstrong creature – banding together to further a suspect cause is truly chastening. Plainly, Ms.ery loves company. This is the hidden agenda (or agendera) behind much of what passes for both literary production and controversy in our intensely politicized climate and, I suspect, has infiltrated the unconscious gradients of the present debate as well. The same is true for what we might call multicultural tokenism, which ensures that one or another mode of presumed social displacement reflected in origin, complexion or locality will deputize for good writing itself. But these are all forms of mere adjectivity. What we should be concerning ourselves with is eloquence and vision, talent and responsibility, with noble and memorable poetic utterance wherever it may be found, with a *genuine* colloquial gift of the phrase, and with the keenness and clarity of thought that comes, as Lampman tells us, when leaning pastorally at rest in the sloped shadow of our hats – not when strutting for Pamela Wallin or posing for the literary pages or indulging in putative subtleties of perception and affect akin, as you may recall from *The Summoner's Tale*, to dividing a fart into twelve equal parts with a cartwheel. The words of Sinperlavio Ivo, the national poet of Botswana, would apply here as well, illustrating that there exists an essential poetic commitment that cuts across traditions. Ivo wrote in his *Diaries of a Tracker*: 'Mastery of language is as seldom found as good, cooked fish but ideologies are common as boiled milk. We should remember that hot fish sticks to the ribs, hot milk to the pan.'

I used to be an avid reader of current Canadian verse until I discovered that it stuck to the pan rather than to the ribs. And in fact, it ultimately came to impress me as a kind of oxymoron. Rather than making me 'twice alive', as you maintain of the art in general, I found that it left me almost half dead. What Rex Murphy once wrote in his weekly newspaper column about political life in this country – 'The problem with Canadian politics is not a surplus of elites, but a tidal wave of mediocrities' – is equally true of our poetry. On the plus side, though, I do find it to be most effective as a cure for insomnia: ten minutes of Janis Rapoport, Christopher Dewdney, Kate Braid, Steve McCaffery or Bronwen Wallace and I am out like a light. If Canadian poetry were written in the U.S. it would by this time have been packaged and exported as a potent sedative at considerable profit to all. Just take one or two poems at bedtime as needed. But when it comes to staying awake, I confine my intensive and serious reading of Canadian *poets* to the handful in our midst who have something to say and the verbal means to say it with. Making a case for poetic recuperations, you lament: 'And so many things are lost.' Would to God a few more things were.

-------

AUTHOR'S NOTE: This is the unexpurgated and subsequently revised version of a letter published in the *Montreal Gazette* for July 14, 1999. It was intended as a rebuttal to Lorna Crozier's article of the week before in 'The Writing Life' column, entitled 'Poetry flourishes best against the odds'. The original letter was printed over Ms. Crozier's response to it which began, somewhat disingenuously, 'Who is David Solway?', proceeded to answer the rhetorical question by opining that said Solway must be 'some kind of minor academic' (rather than, say, Lamont Cranston), went on to condemn said minor academic's 'sad example of the old colonial attitude that undermines anything authentically of this place', and concluded with a roster of apparently superb contemporary Canadian poets that the old colonialist, assuming he had not yet 'doddered off into retirement', should brush up on before 'he dares to face a Canadian classroom again'. Naturally David Solway, now that he had been exposed by Ms. Crozier's deft riposte, was shaken to the core, but a good dosage of Roo Borson, Jan Zwicky, Patrick Friesen and Susan Musgrave, all of whom figured on Ms. Crozier's list, had the inevitable tranquillizing effect, leading to a good night's sleep and equanimity regained.

# THE MONTREAL FORTIES

LET ME BEGIN with a conditional. *If* one accepts that Canadian poetry actually *matters* and that it has a valid role to play on the world stage – by no means a self-evident proposition according to Michael Harris, writing in a recent issue of *Montreal Review of Books* – *then* it follows that the poetic and critical ferment of the Montreal forties demands our attention and respect. For Montreal in that explosive decade was the crucible in which the elements of a national poetry were mixed and the various movements agitating the international scene were distilled and domesticated for home production. Many of the major poets in the country were here – A. M. Klein, P. K. Page and Irving Layton among the most prominent – and the debate over theory and prosody that was to furnish the gradients of a modernist (and eventually a post-modernist) agenda was opened in the pages of *Preview* and *First Statement*, the incunabula of fiery exchanges, of poetic tumult and reflection in Canada in this century. All this would suggest that Brian Trehearne's meticulously researched and intricately reasoned *The Montreal Forties* is long overdue and that we owe its author a debt of gratitude for having redeemed belatedness.

Among the themes that he treats are the question of what, for the poets of the time, constituted the principle of a poem's unity, the troubled marriage with the Imagist imperative of fragmentation and dissonance, and 'the decade's difficulties in grappling with the force of modernist impersonality in an era demanding intense personal commitments'. Trehearne leads us with deft assurance through the antinomies and paralogisms of that formative period, the clash of personalities associated with the competing schools (Aestheticist vs Proletarian, Academic vs Progressive, Formalist vs Experimental) and the constant sparring with the long shadows cast by world-class poets like Eliot, Pound and Auden who set the terms of the debate. His purpose, though, is essentially conciliatory. 'We have not been really interested in the experiences that bound these poets together,' he laments, 'only in those that alienated them.' Wishing to redress the balance, Trehearne attempts instead to discover what all these polemicists and competitors had in common, in order to build a critical understanding 'that evokes new commonalities and sees through the local animosities of the period.'

This is doubtless a noble aim in the abrasive and logomachic environment of Montreal poetry in particular and Canadian poetry in general, a state of 'poetomachia' in which we are still implicated. If the poetic climate in this country is not especially notable for the consistent production of undeniable excellence, it is certainly qualified by a predilection for conflict and a passion for declamatory animadversion. Charting the careers of important editorial figures like Patrick Anderson and John Sutherland and comparative luminaries like Klein, Page, Dudek and Layton, Trehearne tries to show that underlying all the polemics that divided (and continue to divide) us there are nevertheless certain factors of consensus at work: namely, that we are all labouring to survive and even prosper in a small parochial country the larger world has tended to regard with sublime indifference (as Michael Schmidt, editor of Carcanet in England, recently put it, Canadian poetry is a 'short street'), and that the issues and positions that set us against one another *are not so much substantive as political*. No particular movement (or poet) enjoys a lien on the 'reality' which poetry presumably mediates, identifies or inscribes. Much of the controversy that distracts us is ostensibly a question of what happens to be 'locally fashionable' or is merely the concussion of 'fruitless and transitory tastes'. The truth, so far as Trehearne sees it, is that the price we pay for continued dissension is at times confiscatory and that in any case we have far more in common than we might initially have considered.

Formalists have experimented with free verse. Urban poets have published pastoral works. The impersonal voice grows urgently insistent and personal. Working-class manifestants are suddenly found writing in the marmoreal and classical modes. Antagonists like Sutherland and Anderson are approximately reconciled. Allies like Dudek and Layton become dedicated adversaries. If the lines sundering one theoretical position from another turn out to be porous or wavering and are crossed and recrossed in complete disregard of supposedly rooted affiliations (Layton and Dudek more or less patched things up in later age), then it would appear to follow that these eristic and conceptual borders are largely artificial constructs and that we would be better served to determine what unites rather than separates us. Perhaps Trehearne is right in his critical instincts and the brawls in which we habitually engage amount to little more than a tempest in a jigger of Caribou rotgut. In fact, as poets struggling for credibility in a small-market community at the margins of the greater world, we may benefit from a kind of paradoxical freedom to pursue our own ends without having to take dictation from anyone (as Borges argued was the prerogative of the Argentinian writer, whose relation to Spain and its continental neighbours resembles our own susceptiveness to England and the U.S.). Trehearne's efforts to demonstrate what binds rather than severs, while tracking the development of both our poetry and our poetics in the creative hotbed that Montreal was (and is once again), deserve recognition, however sceptical some may feel.

Thus *The Montreal Forties* does not take sides in our homegrown disputes or offer to defend one standpoint at the expense of another. Censure or contestation forms no part of the author's intention and indeed would violate the premises on which the book is raised, which are those of historical awareness and present accommodation. The downside of this approach is that the book generally lacks acerbic bite and distinctive flair, although this is understandable in the circumstance. Like Baby Bear's porridge, the rhetorical temperature is remarkably even, which makes for an edible if at time slightly monotonous collation. The only other cavil I have is that Trehearne sometimes writes as if poets were driven exclusively by theoretical concerns rather than by the immediacies of their experience. I am not minimizing the importance of theory, which at the very least serves as a pretext for bracing scraps between poets and helps them to mark out their territory, validate their appetites or even rationalize their limitations. But theory usually comes in after the fact, as a form of justification for temperamental inclination or visceral impulse, and is then carried back to the beginning of the writing process, occupying a prior status it rarely merits. Trehearne tends to forget that despite the often spectacular clash of theoretical positions and dispositions, the poetry comes before the poetics and the response precedes the reason. His is a misconception common to the academic mindset whose competence is analytic and *post hoc* rather than orphic and *in medias res*. The consummation of the 'insurgent blood' (to quote Layton) which drives the poet is entirely foreign to his perspective.

In the last analysis, *The Montreal Forties* may, I suspect, be good for us, even if, like many things that are good for us, it is somewhat lacking in variety and spice. Still, it is a book well worth reading and assimilating.

# READING RICHARD OUTRAM

> I batter upward
> spiral to lightblaze in rare air
> – 'Dove Legend'

I WOULD LIKE TO LIKE the poetry of Richard Outram more than I do. I admire his craft and technical aplomb, his nobility of purpose and largeness of vision, his sense of a tradition that animates and supports, the opulence of his means. His most recent book, *Dove Legend*, is in parts a veritable *tour de force* and fulfils the promise made to the reader in earlier works like *Man in Love*, *Hiram and Jenny* and *Mogul Recollected*. That's the good news. And it is very good news indeed. The reader can only feel grateful for the lyric sensitivity and emotional depth of poems such as '"*after the waterbrooks*"' in which the poet registers the dual nature of fire, the sun that flares upon the 'kindled water' of a pool over which he bends to drink and the 'image of a naked napalmed child' coming together in his mind, so that

> … in the same
> Conflagration I straighten to proclaim
> that nothing is negated in the world.

But there is bad news too. Despite (or maybe because of) the eminence and magnitude one intuits in his oeuvre, the propensity for risk-taking which is his signature, reading Outram is a bit like navigating the Clashing Rocks that bedevil epic latitudes. As often as not I'm not quite sure what he is talking about or even how he contrives in a given poem to get from one passage to another. Sometimes the logical connectives between stanzas, no matter how deliberately implicit, seem severely underworked. At other times I find that he errs on the side of extravagance, that he grows just a little too florid and rhetorically unmitigated for comfort, a characteristic that consorts with the fuzziness of voice one occasionally detects. (Since you have so much to say, say it clearly! the irascible part of me cries out.) I also note an unfortunate tendency to the painful pun or inverted cliché – 'the taught line', 'knot-quite', 'the burning ambush', 'the heart of darkest America', 'where there's hope there's death', 'make a necessity of virtue' – as well as to the occasional archaism – 'parlous', 'perforce', 'save' for 'except' – that even a possible irony of intent does not wholly amortize. One must try to be scrupulous here. Peter Sanger's assessment in article and book that 'Richard Outram is one of the best poets in the language' and Alberto Manguel's back cover blurb to the identical effect, namely that 'Richard Outram is one of the finest poets in the English language', are plainly a trifle stentorian. The fact is that Richard Outram is one of the more interesting poets in Canada when he is writing at the *hauteur de sa tâche*.

I confess then to a feeling of guilt in letting a periodically unfavourable reaction to his work register so starkly, especially when I consider all the drivel and gloop one has to contend with in the poetry of this country. And I am aware that the ambivalence with which I approach his work may seriously compromise the deposition I wish to make in his behalf. But on second thought, perhaps this curious state of equivocation is not all that rare and many readers of poetry will surely have found themselves in the position of recognizing a poet's value while respondingly cautiously on the level of personal taste. I would candidly acknowledge, as a case in point, that T. S. Eliot is a major and possibly *necessary* poet, yet I cannot read him without dismay. Thankfully, I find the situation far more agreeable when it comes to Richard Outram and my dismay is tempered with delight to see technics and effusiveness pulling in tandem.

So let me state, this time for the record, that I regard Outram as a poet capable of soaring to genuine heights and one remarkable among his national contemporaries, but the downside of his gift is that he does tend to suffer now and again from a paradoxical condition of acute rhetorical laryngitis combined with the inability to stop talking. One finds oneself wishing, for example, that his Regina Clarissima, Queen of the Soapsuds, had drowned in her bath rather than be allowed the coloratura prattle of

Baleful Ambassadors, kicking stiletto heels
in rococo ante-rooms, clutching their bulls;
boffins brandishing facsimile blueprints
of daft perpetual patent emotion machines;
Bishops with schemes for the greater fleecing
of sheep to the glory of indigent Mammon;
flogging Rear-Admirals spoiling to pillage
the fabulous innocent Sacrosanct Islands.
– 'Scorn from the Throne'

Even the studied attempt at mockery in jingle-time does not redeem the
poem from a kind of bathos, a sense of overproduction not consonant
with its presumed intended effect. This over-the-top quality is a staple of
Outram's poetic sensibility, which might well be only the obverse of a
brimming verbal endowment. The problem is how to come to terms
with the uneven aspect of the work in general, which often tends to read
as if it were perhaps too benignly edited or too indulgently conceived. I
suspect that he finds the impetus to write irresistible, that he has diffi-
culty bringing himself to stop when a poem is actually finished or rest-
ing for very long between volumes to give both reader and poet a chance
to recover their resources, so that one sometimes gets the impression of
a long freight train of words, lines, stanzas, poems and books blocking
the crossings. Outram's reader, whether casual or dedicated, requires
enormous patience.

And yet, despite my hesitations and caveats, there is no doubt that
Outram is an exceptionally talented poet – at any rate, when his motor is
running. In reading the best of his work I am often reminded of a pas-
sage from Thomas Moore's *Meditations* (not the eighteenth-century
Irish poet but the New Age spiritualist): 'Living one point after another
is one form of experience, and it can be emphatically productive. But
stopping for melisma gives the Soul its reason for being.' Melisma refers
to a group of notes sung on a single syllable, to the ornamentation of a
musical phrase, and in general to the variations made possible by a
supervening template. In poetry it implies incremental repetition,
metaphorical epithet, emotional intensification and especially metrical
interpolations. Consider as illustration the following poem of three
rhyming quatrains, entitled 'Bedroom'.

Light, by stealth, at last has occupied
The citadels and forests thus made plain,
The intricacy frost has ramified,
Our mingled breath condensed upon the pane

Of simple glass that keeps us from the night;
And in which after dark, returned by chance,
Darkened reflection offered us the sight
Of all our naked likeness at a glance.

I waken, still enamoured, given pause
By you, my deeply sleeping wife,
The certainty of death, as a lost cause,
The luminous unlikelihood of life.

This is a bijou lyric if ever there was one, concluding in a line that elements itself in the memory, 'the luminous unlikelihood of life'. If, as I believe, a poem lives in the power of the phrase, riveting a thought or feeling or a sudden, fleeting awareness securely in the mind in virtue of apt or incantatory formulation, then Outram has stopped for melisma in this piece, pulling off a small miracle and strengthening his bid for what every poet passionately desires: survival by language.

Unlike the example provided by so many of his peers in which tenderness collapses into either sentimentality or banality, Outram manages here to turn a lurking platitude into a rich and resonant insight, giving us a poem as packed and intricate as a microchip. Observe the double effect of imaginative range and technical virtuosity, which save 'Bedroom' from the besetting vice of mere self-expression to which confessional poets in particular are disablingly prone: a patterned rhyme scheme leavened by adroit enjambment (lines 1, 4, 7, and 9) which locks the poem into place while at the same time moderating insistence; the subtle interpolation of the celebrated glass-darkly image from Corinthians 1:13, as Manguel has noted in his intelligent paraphrase of the poem (*Globe and Mail*, April 22, 2000); the median Old-English four-beat measure varied intermittently – three beats in the third line and, of course, in the closure to set it off rhythmically; the echoing spondees that clinch lines 2 and 11 ('made plain' /

'lost cause'), thus accentuating the pathos of its subject; the skilfully cambered diction generating what is referred to above as the power of the phrase; and a faint background iambic metre so diversified as to keep the poem from congealing into predictability, into likelihood. The last line is a metrical feat, in which weak, nonsequential monosyllables quietly introduce the slow, reflective, waltz-like dactyls that culminate in the benchmark iamb, reinforcing both the differential stress and aphoristic energy I have pointed to. What we have is a sort of wedding dance consummated in the two inevitables of the night: love and death. (Or rather, death and love, reminiscent of another fine poem, 'Barbed Wire', in which a startling juxtaposition between a wedding band and a barbed-wire fence brings out the knowledge of 'death, bright entanglement, and troth.') In this way, by using all the means at its disposal, the poem achieves the condition of memorability.

Only an authentic poet could accomplish something like this, and indeed the success is sufficiently repeated to establish Outram as a vintage if intermittent Parnassian. His 'Diapason in *Thimble Theatre*', to take only one more instance, is another moving poem that strives to negotiate 'love's ingenious carnalities' even though 'none shall tell/the stricken mysteries of Souls that juxtapose.' An unstanchable Muse does not always augur well, yet we encounter enough such well-turned pieces in his summa volume and partial retrospective, *Dove Legend*, to permit conviction to triumph on the whole over doubt.

One more thing. It becomes clear as we grapple to assimilate these complex and involuted poems, these decantings of language poured from a height (for even the bawdy is consciously, perhaps a little too consciously, wrought), that Outram must be taken on his own terms. He is not a fashionable poet – we recall Ian Hamilton's definition of fashion as 'one of oblivion's most reliable lieutenants' – which speaks to the likely durability of his finest work as it does to its singularity. And it is this singularity – 'beware,' he slyly warns in 'Admonition, *Ipse Dixit*, from Afar', 'of the first person singular' – which may explain the uncommon demands it places on its readers, whose struggle to master his laminated pages may feel at times equal to the poet's. As he writes in 'Philosopher',

... this
exacts a prodigious toll,
which he insisted can only
be paid in kind.

In conclusion, I concede the possibility that Outram is the kind of poet one must learn to read in the way one gradually masters a foreign language and that the discomfort readers like me sometimes feel with portions of his work is arguably a function of initial labour, of the rigours of acquisition. If this is so, it is a feature in the art of reading Richard Outram that would certainly account for the occasional uneasiness and ambiguity of one's response. Meanwhile there are always those cynosure pieces that, resembling his own Adam in 'Evidence in the Garden', help us to 'Slip into the fallow / Habitable world' with something like gratitude for the 'fallen light unfurled'.

# THE GREAT DISCONNECT

Plain prose, today I want to write plain prose. I want to write,
'Yesterday, the sun didn't come up & hoar frost clung to trees.'
— Roberta Rees, 'Hoar Frost'

It is more true a scabious
field than it is a pretty
meadow
— Charles Olson, 'Maximus, to Gloucester, Sunday, July 19'

Greek athletes, bushy satyrs, figgy nymphs,
some set of the artist's inner circle
making it where everyone failed to make it.
— Peter Van Toorn, 'Swinburne's Garden'

'Engage!' — Captain Jean-Luc Picard, *Star Trek: The Second Generation*

# Introductory

POPE'S INTERLOCUTOR in 'The First Satire of the Second Book of Horace' facetiously objects that in refusing to name his targets except via antonomasia or classical aliases, the poet is actually doing more damage than he intended.

> The fewer still you name, you wound the more;
> Bond is but one, but Harpax is a score.

By these lights I am being both prudent and decorous in singling out individual poets – Bonds, not Harpaxes – for explicit commentary and denunciation, comparing them openly with their betters and giving reasons and demonstrations. I have let myself be guided by three principles in working up an approximate set of what I think of as matching incompatibles: 1) my negative samples must be representative; 2) they must be pretty well recognizable; and 3) they should be determined to an important degree by the countervailing instances of good writing I have been able to find.

These thermostatic moments are predicated on motifs of intimacy – consanguineous, sexual, affiliate, communal – to serve as metaphorical correlate for the theme of attachment and relation, of connecting with a source and a destination, that I will be developing. The good poets I am seeking to serve as 'opposite numbers' to the mediocrities are those possessing what Les Murray in the poem of that title calls 'sprawl,' that centred and venturesome quality of mind which, 'Reprimanded and dismissed / ... listens with a boot up on the rail / of possibility', and also 'occurs in art, the fifteenth to twenty-first / lines in a sonnet, for example'. (One thinks of Milton, among the most sprawling of our poets, whose caudated sonnets exceeded the standard number of lines.) Sprawl is thus the attribute of a sensibility that is founded in stable forms – both personal and aesthethic – but is at the same time capable of varying and complexifying them at will.

What I am afraid of is that the divide between, let's say, sprawl and slump, confident saunter and lemming plummet, between the nobility and wonder of the poetic quest and the abuses and shabbiness of its current practice threatens now to become entrenched. I am afraid, too, that the time for recognition and response is quickly running out. A little longer and we will have forgotten that good poetry may still be possible or indeed that it ever existed in the first place. I believe the only way to counter this drift is to cease trading in the usual velleities and placebos that double for criticism in today's literary environment and embark on a process of audits and disclosures to reveal the real value of most of the work now being mass-produced. Anything else is only a way of evading responsibility.

# 1.

IT IS NO SECRET that the popular benchmark of aesthetic discernment is notoriously low: house music, pictorial copies of nature, formula novels and newspaper elegies would seem to embody the average level of aesthetic taste in music, painting, fiction and poetry. To rely on such a standard would plainly spell the end of the arts. On the other hand, the wiredrawn and overly convoluted *theoretical* preoccupations of the vanguard moderns and their postmodern successors have created an aesthetic state of affairs more or less incomprehensible to anyone who is not a specialist in the field. This might explain why those who have not benefited from a university education in the arts must remain baffled and resentful before the compositions of John Cage, the painting of Mark Rothko, the fiction of Samuel Beckett and the poetry of Ezra Pound – to name only a sparse few among the purveyors of aesthetic darkness in our time. As for poetry, it now tends to manifest either as *written speech* or as *encrypted prose*, the first appealing largely to the indolent and the second to the pedantic, the two major constituencies of practising poets who, as I will argue, pretty well comprise their own readership. In either case the appeal is to the inner circle. And this situation is likely to continue as the Great Disconnect between poetry and a relatively discerning *nonspecialist* readership is increasingly reinforced by the academy and the coterie.

The question of the poet's readership is obviously not a simple one. It seems to me that we can distinguish four separate, real or imaginary (but variously efficacious) destinations for poetry, notwithstanding the era in which it is being written. To some degree the poet always writes to or for her peers and congeners who, as a gallery of critics, promoters, editors, reviewers and fellow practitioners, form her immediate, professional entourage. But I would maintain energetically that this audience is the least important – except pragmatically – of the diverse addresses poets envisage for their work. For poets always harbour a shadowy post office in their imagination and compose and mail their poems like letters to an ideal respondent or correspondent who may not exist in any verifiable way or who may exist only potentially. One such destination consists of the poet's ancestors and precursors with whom he may be engaged in some sort of adversarial relation à la Bloom or whom he approaches in a posture of reverence and frank indebtedness, inscribing his poems in the repertory they have assembled. Another – in my estimation, probably the single most compelling and momentous addressee – is Divinity itself, from whom I am convinced many poets secretly believe they have received their gift and talent and who remains the final and sanctioning recipient of the work. Aside from consanguinity with the major biblical prophets – those godfathers of inspiration – which poets have been known to trumpet now and then, the traditional affinity here if it is genuinely felt and not mere self-inflation is with Caedmon of Whitby who, as the Venerable Bede explains, 'did not acquire the art of poetry from men or through any human teachers but received it as a free gift from God. For this reason he could never compose any frivolous or profane verses …' but was constrained or inspired to sing Creation. Talent is donative and demands reciprocity.

But apart from the empirical syndicate of coevals, the illustrious dead and the bestowing Transcendent, there is a fourth audience, that made up of educated or sympathetic 'common readers' without whom the poet must reconcile himself or herself to a profound and ascetic solitude akin to lifelong meditation or prayer. There have been poets throughout history – Emily Dickinson comes immediately to mind – who have saluted or embraced this solitary, anchoritic existence but most of us, as frail and desiring human beings, need at least potential contact or intimacy with a living readership. The desideratum is that this should be or – to defer to the reality principle – *be imagined as* a general (or composite) readership, Paul Celan's 'addressable thou', now or in posterity, to sustain the sense of a nurturing community and to validate the work.

I think there is little doubt that at the present time the majority of poets have forfeited any fruitful relationship with two of the crucial 'audiences' I have identified, eschewing the past as a burden and impediment and dismissing any possible lay audience of able and interested nonspecialists as a mere irrelevance. Of their connection with the Divine, nothing can be said – let us hope the lines of this revivifying communion have not been entirely severed or attenuated. But it is the readership of peers, literary sophisticates, critical backers and corporate patrons that remains the designated target and accounts in large measure for the unexigent or cryptic nature of the work they insist on producing and the ablative sensibility from which it flows.

So far as I can see, the only way out of this dilemma is to posit someone like the fourth interlocutor, the mythical 'common reader' who is not common at all but, as I have suggested, an educated or sympathetic nonspecialist, even if such readers scarcely, no longer or do not yet exist. For the lack of this *uncommon* 'common reader' is painfully the case in poetry, which lost whatever currency or diffusion it once enjoyed with the onset of the First World War and underwent a concomitant loss of faith in the moral and intellectual viability of an entire civilization with the Second. (Mallarmé quipped that poetry took a wrong turn after Homer, but the dereliction is far more recent – perhaps after Mallarmé.) As the world careened through the twentieth century and experienced critical impact with a revived barbarism, it suffered many significant casualties, among which the poetic imagination was one of the most grievous if least lamented – especially in the complacent and privileged West where poetry and social/political resistance were profoundly estranged from one another. (The current spate of anti-war or anti-American poetry falls into a different category of protest. It is of the *permissible* variety, an expression of popular sentiment that runs no risks and merely reinforces a broad, social status quo, in many countries right up to the highest levels of government, rather than opposing it.)

As a sympathetic and educated readership fell away, establishing the conditions of the Great Disconnect, the poet was left in a cultural vacuum that could be filled only in part and variably sustained by the life-support system offered by the university. In this way began the unholy alliance between the poet and the academic, the one feeding off the other in symbiotic futility. Poets began to write for the professors and indeed were more often than not professors themselves. Moreover, deprived of an authentic audience, *poets began to write primarily for one another*, to engage in theoretical wrangles that were as contorted as they were immaterial, to conjure shadowy and ethereal prosodic innovations that no interested layperson could plausibly hope to understand or care about, and to justify their practice by passing themselves off as the self-elected custodians of a vanished intellectual culture, relishing their standing as an elite cohort of cutting-edge sensibilities dealing with matters of exceeding subtlety. The myopia from which we suffer now seems to have reached epidemic proportions as even the critics and professors have entered the loop and inserted themselves into the internal colloquy, happily engaged in the anointment of impostors.

Thus Sam Solecki, an otherwise respectable academic, has elevated Al Purdy to world-class prominence, naively comparing him with the likes of Yeats and not realizing the damage he is thereby inflicting on his candidate for greatness; Harold Bloom, generally an astute reader, has put his money on John Ashbery (as have Donald Barthelme and John Malcolm Brinnin, from whom one might have expected a certain aesthetic sobriety); the anonymous and unsearchable scouts of the prestigious MacArthur Foundation have selected Anne Carson as the recipient of a $500,000 cash award; and booty queen Helen Vendler for her part has endowered the ineffable Jorie Graham. Purdy is a national icon and Ashbery the longtime darling of the conventicles, so there might be some ancillary if unlikely reason to browse intermittently, but can one frankly conceive of any intelligent middlebrow reader spending an evening with Anne Carson or Jorie Graham in the way that my neighbour, a retired engineer, reads Housman and Hardy and listens to recordings of Dylan Thomas? Answer honestly. (Interestingly, poet and critic Christian Wiman, in a recent *Sewanee Review*, alludes directly to Ashbery and Graham as 'would-be great poets' whose work comprises 'endless little cul-de-sacs of consciousness into which fewer and fewer readers are willing to crawl'.)

Naturally the poets will claim that they are at the forefront of artistic renewal and that the opacity or difficulty or prosaicism or just the all-round unsatisfactoriness of their poems, which people like me complain about, is merely apparent. They will see themselves as the purveyors of novelty and experimentation, as a detachment of 'rebel angels' moving away from the old and shopworn – from Hardy and Housman and Thomas – and courageously exploring the new and unique, countering reactionary intransigence and preserving in the process the very foundations of the art. Clearly, the instinct for renovation is built into every discipline or else nothing would ever change. And genuine renewal is assuredly to be admired and encouraged. But the propensity towards posturing and delusion and indulgence is also built in and there may well be periods when shallowness and incompetence are more likely than not to pass themselves off as a kind of creative sublimity beyond the capacity of merely intelligent men and women to recognize and grasp. The issue for our time and with respect to my subject is not between the comparative merits of, for example, A. E. Housman and Jorie Graham as representatives of the old and the new but between the legion of poets like Jorie Graham and the handful of poets like Michael Lind, that is, between poetic ineptitude taken as the necessary obscurity that theoretically goes with any spearheading enterprise and poetic aptitude unafraid of being comprehensible. Making it new, especially by fiat and slogan, is not always making it well and to assume that one leads inexorably to the other is only to ratify what has become a vulgar misconception.

But after a half century and counting of a condition in which poetic prominence is certified by public oblivion, we find ourselves today in the absurd and untenable position delineated above, one in which presumed innovation is a stalking horse for vacuousness and received ideas deputize for stalwart thinking among those who are presumed to know. The Great Disconnect has never been more evident and would account for the fact that there are no more than a dozen or fifteen poets on the entire North American continent who can write meaningful, beautiful or creditable poetry. If poetry did not live intravenously off the agenda-dominated award network and the government-funded but usually indiscriminate granting system (which arrived in Canada in the late fifties to supplement the academy), it would expire immediately, neither with a bang nor a whimper but in a glazed, catatonic silence. (Of bang, more to come.) For the contemporary survival of our poets is predicated almost completely on factors that have little or nothing to do with poetry.

One of the most important of these factors is quasi-political. In other words, poets must attach themselves to allegedly civic causes and ideologies, as representatives of the national mandate or of a supposed communal identity, in order to qualify as aspirants for public largesse and official attention. In Canada particularly, it is almost as if the poets have received a commission to write *cadastrally*, to furnish a register for ideological levy, or to create a fictional past in which to root a respectable future, of which the most conspicuous examples are Margaret Atwood's *The Journals of Susanna Moodie* and Dennis Lee's *Civil Elegies*, especially this latter where passages like

> I know
> the dead persist in
> buildings, by-laws, porticos – the city I live in
> is clogged with their presence; they
> dawdle about in our lives and form a destiny, still
> incomplete, still dead weight, still
> demanding whether Canada will be ...

display themselves impenitently as *poetry*. This prosy, declamatory sort of writing that reads almost like historiography is now pervasive and, in fact, we cannot escape it wherever we may turn. For we are haunted, especially in Canada, by our craving for ancestors, for 'the ghosts that used to rise when you, a child, crossing / the dyke from BC Packers, night, saw, Out of the dark this strange / white light,' as Daphne Marlatt struggles to put it. Increasingly, this convention of the art has been inflected by a bizarre state-driven multiculturalism that is having the effect of diversifying and multiplying the number of *faux-semblant* ancestors now teeming in the ideological atmosphere, like lemures liberated from the tomb.

Meanwhile our poets dress themselves up as renovators of the language without whom, presumably, people would be reduced to carrying out their ordinary discourse in grunts and pantomimes, like the speculators of Lagado. The contradiction here is that many of these same poets have *already* valorized common speech as the register in which they blithely continue to work. Collaterally, in succumbing to the lure of an *ostensibly* simplified language which speaks to ordinary men and women, they have committed both an act of dissimulation and an act of violence, for life's great simplicities will often grow inordinately muddled in their reticulations, interferences and conflicts with one another. Reflective people demand more of their poets and resent being patronized. As Geoffrey Hill claims in a recent interview in *The Paris Review*, 'such simplification of language – what one might call a kind of mass demotic – is gripped by its own oxymoron; purporting to be accessible, it is in fact haughty and condescending, because it will not respect the intelligence of those from whom it demands a response.' As for the more delphically inclined among our poets, they are mainly preoccupied in convincing themselves (and others) that they are the bearers of the visionary imagination in a commercially sordid and technologically profane society, that they are voices crying in the wilderness rather than pontificating in the lecture hall. Their effect on public as well as educated taste is equally pernicious where or when it is felt.

A plague on both their houses, one might be tempted to sputter, until one realizes it is all really one house containing competing branches of the same family business. Simplifiers or complicators, they are everywhere around us, clustering in the creative writing departments of the universities where they accept a salary for effectively obfuscating the discipline, or congregating in publicly endowed organizations, like the League of Canadian Poets, where they exchange addresses, offer one another readings on the usual *quid pro quo* basis, and help determine the winners of the annual literary competitions. The *raison d'être* of such alliances is cronyism, not collegiality. (A case in point: one well-known and influential Canadian poet handpicked a provincial writers' guild jury and then – received the award.) And all the while they continue to bring forth torrents of drivel and fustian while sinking, many of them, into linguistic 'experiments' that would distress even Prostetnic Vogon Jeltz.[1]

Consider once more the material that camouflages itself as poetry these days: blowzy episodic wanderings (Judith Fitzgerald), stringy flitches of prose – and not very good prose at that – veining down the page (Don Summerhayes), idle reveries gaping with an utter lack of substance and urgency (George Bowering), half-baked domestic reflections that belong in a diary where privacy may be expected to preclude embarrassment (Susan Musgrave), insoluble gibberish without any latent or discoverable ordering principle and leading to no appreciable conclusion (Christopher Dewdney), orthographic high jinks which the poet presupposes will repristinate the phonemic structure of the language (bill bissett), approved proletarian sentiment couched in the journalese of hortatory dispatch (Tom Wayman), a fey pretentiousness cloaked in a kind of peregrine orientalism (Douglas Barbour), slightness wedded to garrulity (Don McKay), and lines that seem to have been fed into the chipper-shredder of a mechanical imagination and spewed out to end where they do, nudging toward the right-hand margin, certainly without rhyme, plainly without reason, and manifestly without purpose or effect (bp Nichol).

It should come as no surprise that almost none of this stuff is memorable in whole or in part and cannot justifiably propose to enter the (unsubsidized) anthology of the literature or become an integral part of our cultural literacy. For as the poets continue to write for one another, the poetry gets worse and worse, shedding any *genuine* communal reason for its existence. The only survival it can properly envision is ethnographic and archaeological, as signs and tokens, that is, of an aspect or era in the life of a nation, culture or civilization, like a broken shard or a barely legible temple account or, at best, a Dorset carving. The Great Disconnect has never been more in evidence than today as the schools and cenacles continue to proliferate and the critical megacorp grows ever more powerful.

The negative dynamic I am considering here is what philosopher J. L. Austin analysed as the distance between the constative and referential 'orders of reality'. It is the social assessments and constitutive 'truths' of a community, its collective protocols and judgements, which determine what he denominates as 'illocutionary facility', that is, the texts and statements that enable us to 'enact a collectivity' which posits and establishes what is 'real' even if that is in conflict with observable fact. In our context, this seems especially so, as Yiorgos Chouliaras said in a recent lecture entitled 'Greece and Poetry', when we consider 'the conditions of reception generated by institutions that mediate between writers and audiences', conditions are largely preconcerted.

Similarly, sociologist Erving Goffman examines the inclination toward 'selective disattention' to facts which would otherwise challenge the frame of discourse and perception we take for granted. Thus Bobby Hull scores with one foot in the goaltender's crease but the referee calls it a goal and the wrong team wins the Stanley Cup. (It is only in the case of repeatedly outrageous and media-circulated violations of the Real, as in Olympic skating and World Cup soccer, that people may object, although that is no guarantee of rectification.) The assessment evicts the datum as the record does the occasion. Everyone usually plays along and very few go 'out of frame', accepting an appraisal for a quality or, in the words of philosopher John Searle, an institutional fact for a brute fact. The two may coincide over the long haul, at least in literature where time is the best editor, but in the short run the disjunction is often glaring and egregious. And even time has been known to nod from time to time. The danger is that in certain circumstances the asymmetry between the constative and the referential may persist until, one day, the game ceases entirely to be taken seriously, thanks to the ability of the virtuosos of selective disattention (a.k.a. the credulous or the partisan) to suspend their faculties of critical judgement and to collude in the circulation of propositions and utterances that have little or no dependence on descriptive validity or referential truth. And so the poetasters who litter the scene, even if they are not aware of the paucity of their talents or the impropriety of their pretensions, will continue to be taken at their own evaluation until the constative fiction is exploded or the constative community in question simply disintegrates – which latter is what we may call a condition of perpetual farce.[2]

If poetry is to endure in any real sense, even as one of the minor categories of cultural experience, it must strive to reconnect with its double source of energy and authenticity, namely, with the tradition of forms, themes, principles and hieratic dispositions from which it has cut itself loose,[3] and with a once-and-future readership of noninitiates and, so to speak, cultural amateurs who may eventually be teased back into existence. Most unfortunately, however, the average Canadian (and, perhaps, to a marginally lesser extent, American) poem reads like the minor revelation of a self-exalted psyche, an apocalypse of twitches, reactions, irritations, anxieties, personal recollections, approvals and predilections, centripetal musings and so on, which scant both the repository and the reader.

The trouble is no poet is *so* interesting as a person that he or she can afford to neglect the archive of symbolic forms and patterns. which, infinitely recombinant and expressively universal, rescue the poet from the curse of self-inflation and establish a connection with the generations. But the situation as it now exists produces an entirely scalene relationship between praise and praiseworthiness that could well be fatal to the survival or recrudescence of an authentic poetry. The problem, too, is that those who have acquired celebrity – thus becoming what Naomi Klein calls 'logos' (not *logos*) where social legitimacy substitutes for meaning, truth or talent – are exempt from criticism, appellate proceedings or irreverent thrusts like the one I am attempting in this essay. Fame is like death: once you have entered the condition, you can't be touched, influenced or hurt. Al Purdy and Margaret Atwood are equally safe.

But the marriage or reconciliation between the poet and the reader can only occur in virtue of the very features and properties poetry has broadly renounced: an honest and skilful treatment of the codes and materials of the discipline, which enables the poet to construct a durable artifact (one thinks of Brodsky's maxim, 'a rhyme turns an idea into law'), and an active willingness to postulate, if not to expect, an audience of 'ordinary' but literate readers rather than to transact with a camarilla of dilettantes, adepts and connoisseurs. None of this, regrettably, is happening now. The prophet-figures pass but the mantle falls inevitably to poeticians even less worthy of the innocent reader than the esteemed predecessor was, since taste tends to deteriorate exponentially until finally, blessedly, bottoming out. But this is also why we refuse to give in to terminal despair. For the reign of Chaos and old Night, we would like to believe, can never be total and forever and is always superseded by brief but coruscating periods of cultural resurgence. Or at least such has been the case up to now. The great reckoning may augur differently.

# 2.

TO RETURN TO MY INITIAL CAVEATS. Poetry disconnects from any possible, enlightened and genuinely responsive readership as much when it affects a sort of non-U readability as it does when it pursues the higher unintelligibility or mystification, one tendency being merely the flip side of the other. These are the two standard modes (with some crossover) in which the bulk of our poetry is currently written. In either case, disaster ensues. For whatever poetry may or may not be, it is assuredly neither common speech nor self-infatuated haruspicy, otherwise what would be the point? Here, as an instance of the former bias or trend, is Purdy's chronicle of 'Love at Roblin Lake'.

> My ambition as I remember and
> I always remember was always
> to make love vulgarly and immensely
> as the vulgar elephant doth
> & immense reptiles did
> in the open air openly
> sweating and grunting together
> and going
> 'BOING     BOING     BOING'
> making
> every lunge a hole in the great dark
> for summer cottagers to fall into at a later date
> and hear inside faintly (like in a football
> stadium when the home team loses)
> ourselves still softly
> going
> *'boing     boing     boing'*
> as the vulgar elephant doth
> & immense reptiles did
> in the star-filled places of earth

that I remember we left behind long ago
and forgotten everything ever after
on our journey into the dark

One of the things that has attracted attention to this particular poem is its seemingly daring and unanticipated use of the slang word 'boing,' which explodes on the page with vernacular majuscule-and-italic exuberance and plunks the poem straight down into the purview of all us average folk, as if in anticipation of the word's appropriation by the Nike Shox running shoe commercial. Indeed, Dennis Lee, in the Afterword to the 1986 Collected Purdy, cannot contain himself in his praise for the comic book freshness and restorative unlikelihood of this word, which functions, apparently, as a sign of the 'polyphonic resources' and the precession of the linguistic and perspectival registers, the panning and zooming, he associates with Purdy's methods of composition.[4]

Lee probably forgot that we used to dream about 'boinging' girls when we were about twelve or so and the word was one of the many idiomatic counters we used in order to accommodate our fruitless longing with pretended insouciance. 'Boing' was the predecessor of 'bang,' which I recently heard a performance poet at a local slam hammer away at in a spunky and intrepid exploration of the manifold erotic resources of the language. ('Make the world go BANG!' was the slogan of the 1998 National Poetry Slam in Austin, Texas.) But what either boing or bang, patented as genuine novelty, have to do with poetic language is beyond my conceiving. Rather, what I find in this poem, as in so many others, is a sort of backwards-baseball-cap language, the lackadaisical sublime masquerading as the natively original, Red Green on a rhetorical tear.

Like so many other Purdy lovers, Lee tries to justify the slapdash, unfinished, rough-hewn character of much if not most of the work as somehow *deliberate*, as an illustration of Purdy's desire 'to avoid giving even a sublime poem too much polish.' This might explain some of the curious flaws that tend to mar the piece. Why is the football team losing when in the immediate linear context it should probably be winning or at least holding its own? Why the grammatical solecism in the penultimate line? Why the ampersand? Why the curious slippage from singular to plural when passing from elephant to reptiles – what does the breaking of the parallelism signify? I am not nitpicking here; these are the kinds of details a poet must consider who leaves nothing, not even chance, to chance. One should not try to acquit the incompetent as an instance of creative strategy. Nor, I would hazard, should the poet revise downward, which leads only to the homespun cant we find everywhere substituting for memorable poetic diction.

Here, by contrast, is the first half of Auden's 'Lullaby', a poem machined to narrow tolerances yet describing a similar expansive event.

> Lay your sleeping head, my love,
> Human on my faithless arm
> Time and fevers burn away
> Individual beauty from
> Thoughtful children, and the grave
> Proves the child ephemeral:
> But in my arms till break of day
> Let the living creature lie,
> Mortal, guilty, but to me
> The entirely beautiful.
>
> Soul and body have no bounds:
> To lovers as they lie upon
> Her tolerant enchanted slope
> In their ordinary swoon,
> Grave the vision Venus sends
> Of supernatural sympathy,
> Universal love and hope;
> While an abstract insight wakes
> Among the glaciers and the rocks
> The hermit's sensual ecstasy.

Note how colloquial this poem also sounds, owing chiefly to the deft management of enjambment. But the entire poem is turned on a lathe, with its subtle rhyme scheme, precise syllable count, intricate thematic unfolding (as the reader will note when linking the citation with the remaining two stanzas), and inscription in the tradition, reprising in its second and fortieth lines from one of Wordsworth's 'Lucy' poems the strange use of the word 'human' – 'I had no human fears,' writes the great precursor in an analogous context. (Auden concludes: 'Nights of insult let you pass / Watched by every human love.')

These two passages represent limiting cases, of course, but the Auden poem, in virtue of its language and technique, its aural similarity to, but structural distinctness from, the rhythms and architecture of everyday speech, is readily memorizable whereas the former is not. Nor should we make the mistake of the myriad reviewers and commentators who gratuitously assume that the much-lauded 'simple', 'lively' and 'redemptive' language of Purdy's Make-the-word-go-BOING-type poetry somehow reverberates in the barometric deeps of the mind. Rather, the resolute simple-mindedness and linguistic Jell-O associated with the *attempted* profound is really a species of what Pope in *Peri Bathous* calls 'the Infantine', which is 'when a poet grows so simple, as to think and talk like a child'. (Pope's examples are from Ambrose Philips, but it should be obvious that we suffer no dearth of equally sad instances among our own tribally elected laureates.)

But if poetry is not common speech, neither is it encrypted prose or a kind of butchered semiolect that, everything considered, is often about as comprehensible as a pakapoo ticket. John Ashbery, whose preputial muse tends frequently to deflect his critical judgement, begins his 'Poem in Three Parts' as follows:

> Once I let a guy blow me.
> I kind of backed away from the experience.
> Now years later, I think of it
> Without emotion…

which is at least decipherable if verbally insipid, uninspired and iru-matic. He then proceeds, after informing us that 'Feelings are important' and that 'Mostly I think of feelings, they fill up my life,' to focus, metaphorically no doubt, on

> Nameless shrubs running across a field
> That didn't drain last year and
> Isn't draining this year to fall short
> Like waves at the end of a lake,
> Each with a little sigh,

which leads next to the important question

> Are you sure this is what the pure day
> With its standing light intends?

And we are deep in Ashbery-land, without sense or contour, inchoate, portentous, devoid of coordinates by which we can locate ourselves but learning nevertheless, as a kind of dividend, I suppose, for sticking with the poem as long as we have, that 'the day fries, with a fine conscience' and that 'The conscience is to you as what is known.' The third section slides into its peroration by deposing that

> The time is darker
> For fast reasons into everything, about what concerns it now.
> We could sleep together again but that wouldn't
> Bring back the profit of these dangerous dreams of the sea ...

And so on. This sort of thing, I submit, despite the occasional self-conscious coltishness we find in poems like 'Self-Portrait in a Convex Mirror', is not much help to the bewildered reader. It is, to rephrase Eliot, more like a raid on the articulate than a disengagement of meaning, and certainly an offence to anyone hoping to find the cadenced and patterned language of poetry which offers to become an intrinsic part of what we remember and think, of that which is not 'beyond remembering' (the title of Purdy's final volume). As J. V. Cunningham contends in his seminal 'The Problem of Form', poetry is encoded in form and metre or some memory trace thereof, which provides for stability and variation, connection and interest. Try committing the Ashbery poem or even a portion of it to memory and *keeping it there*, the litmus test of poetic value and power and vivacity. Then try something standard by Yeats or Browning and compare.[5]

The Purdy and Ashbery poems deal with the subject of lovemaking, but where is the love of language, the stroking and caressing of the flesh made word, the erotic attention to prosodic detail, the connection with the body of previous poetry, and the happy consummation of meaning in the union of poet and reader that we find in Auden's little gem?

Where is the surprise and delight of, for example, Sharon Olds's agile handling of poetic technique when she asks in 'Sex Without Love', affecting consternation, how lovers may

> come to the   come to the   God   come to the
> still waters, and not love
> the one who came there with them, light
> rising slowly like steam off their joined
> skin?

– reviving the eruptive device patented by William Morris in 'The Defence of Guenevere' ('Ah Christ! If only I had known, known, known') and risked interventionally by Joyce in *Finnegans Wake* ('when hold hard a jiffy', Penguin, p. 170). Or consider the carnal friskiness of the lovers in Peter Van Toorn's 'Swinburne's Garden',

> each pair
> floating home in some uncharted seafield,
> balling away in limbos of their own,
> past Gibraltar,
> out of bluewaves, formal thermos water,
> into the Atlantic's slick haggle of chrome,
> their well-oiled, limber, bloodstormed bodies
> humping to the racket on the downbeats
> of cymbals, flutes, drums and tambourines,
> and moving those butts
> as if some god had spooked their love-guts
> with his darkspined Aegean wine ...

where the very language of the poem enacts and recapitulates its content in a kind of lexical orgy of *distinctive fusions* with the tradition (Swinburne; a tincture of Wallace Stevens' 'Peter Quince at the Clavier'), with the solid, corporeal world that has too often been abandoned by the narcissism of mere personal reportage, and with a sense of vital temporality (the poet as time-binder)? What Van Toorn is repining in this magisterial poem is the

> profane loss
> of due notions: Stamping civilized life
> at an unrecorded distance. Like the loss
> of Stradivarius's recipe for
> violinwood ...

and the correlative disappearance of the poet's 'cocked and loaded self, clicking in energy'. Yet he cannot easily surrender the possibility that the poetic or Stradivarian music continues to survive somewhere, in Swinburne's garden maybe, or mysterious 'as a credit card lodged with Whitman's hat / on the Atlantic's bottom'. And that the lovers, now 'reduced to a legendary jumble / of arms, legs, genitals', may yet remain 'electric as cables taking a phone call / through the mummy-slime of arctic currents.'

But connections are more often lost and broken than established. Jan Zwicky, who won the 1999 Governor General's Award for her *Songs for Relinquishing the Earth*, is equipped with a strong sense of the poetic line and the ability to turn out the random 'language moment'. But she is nevertheless limited to the reproduction of identical effects, her poems, irrespective of whatever skill they exhibit, tending to sound like one string vibrating in a tiny breeze. In a long meandering piece entitled 'The Geology of Norway', she delivers what might be her hallmark dirge-*cum*-aspiration, her elegy for the living, which inadvertently sums up the poet's predicament and the brief I am arguing.

> Being, I have come to think,
> is music; or perhaps
> it's silence. I cannot say.
> Love, I'm pretty sure,
> is light.
>   You know, it isn't
> what I came for, this bewilderment
> by beauty. I came
> to find a word, the perfect
> syllable, to make it reach up,
> grab meaning by the throat
> and squeeze it till it spoke to me.

How else to anchor
meaning?

Despite the subvocal intimations of music that either cinch or trouble these excerpted lines, depending on your take (I am reminded of Glenn Gould humming beneath his piano in his recital of Mozart's sonatas), what is one to make of the pseudo-philosophical proneness to abstraction ('Being', 'silence', 'Love', 'beauty', 'meaning', 'memory') in a poem that should by rights exert itself to *perform* these concepts in metaphor and rhythm? Or of the cumbrous mummery of its subject? (Being, she has come to think, is, perhaps, silence. After an aperçu of this magnitude, one might be forgiven for putting down the book and taking time off to reread Schopenhauer, where such insights properly accrue and are more profitably addressed.) Or of the peculiar Canadian addiction to bathos? (If you grab meaning by the throat and squeeze – the poetic version of the Shawinigan handshake – it is not likely to speak to you but to splutter, gag and possibly expire.) Or of the standard thematic implication of loss, disconnection and abandonment expressed in a poem that comes 'to find a word, the perfect / syllable' in order to 'anchor / meaning' – yet does so in words and syllables that somehow remain uncabled to the verbal and auditory imagination, drifting away from the concrete realizability that would warrant them and the cultural holograph of poetic form and structure that provides for memory, continuity and relation?

Compare the following untitled section from Carmine Starnino's *Yukon Postcards*, a suite of love poems that work with landscape as a tangible homology for language, providing a description of a panorama that separates the poet from his beloved while simultaneously forming a bridge that links them to one another, precisely as language does. Distance is sometimes a condition of proximity. Taking liberties with the natural order, he plays with the idea of seasonal transpositions and synaesthetic conversions, creating what is a largely imaginary vista of desire and nominative fulfillment, again, precisely as language does.

> The pussywillow's silver windchime
> clatters, the sweet clover is ochre-muted,
> and frost stills the bluebell's clapper.

The cinquefoil's five-note canto is off key;
the larkspur, shy creature, is spooked
into stage fright; and the fireweed's whistle
has been thinned to a bloomless hiss.
Even the sea-susurrus is gone; the wind's now
radio static in the trees, whose leaves
find the colour green hard to pronounce.
But in grass that is a tawny stubble of syllables,
forget-me-nots blue-bugle your name.

Just as in the passage from Zwicky, music, love, meaning and memory abound, but in a profusion of sensible particulars arbitrated in synaesthetic images and mated syllables, the whole surmounting the threat of disjunction by a plush dehiscence of language and a willingness to take risks (the moxie of 'blue-bugle' as a verb, which comes perilously close to a Crashaw-like conceit but stays just this side of it). There is no question of relinquishment here but, quite the contrary, of attachment: to landscape, to words, to the lover who is to receive this bouquet of verses, to the reader who is also the beloved and to whom the poet reaches out with a deference and respect attested by the care he lavishes on the poem, and to the tradition to which the poem couples its recovered melodies and its nuptial longing. The allusion to Keats's 'To Autumn' is unmistakable, and if we listen carefully we will hear, in fugal interlacings of sound and image, Gerard Manley Hopkins' 'Inversnaid' and John Clare's 'To the Sniper', anchoring memory. And memory no less than desire is the nub of the issue. Note the clutch of forget-me-nots (out of season, yet what else?) to clarion the lover's name in the midst of a desolate autumn prospect. And note as well the link to another of Clare's poems – Clare is one of Starnino's poetic teachers – which begins 'Language has not the power to speak what love indites,' yet the 'post-card', culling a floral and recollected music, proceeds to speak it through paradox, analogy and imaginary commutations, precisely as language will.

The relation between Zwicky and Starnino I have plotted is to my way of thinking uncannily reminiscent of that between Anne Michaels and Brent MacLaine, the former a media cynosure and the latter still awaiting the recognition that is his due. Michaels and MacLaine tend to address similar themes – love, memory, separation and retrieval – in a similar mixed style which may be described as in equal parts discursive, narrative and reflective. But the similarities stop there. Like Zwicky, Michaels has her moments and can finesse the occasional good line into paginal space but the work finally comes across as cloying and diffuse, even gabby. Whereas, like Starnino, MacLaine has the knack of memorable phrasing and a talent for strong, glyptic imagery that leaves a complex backscatter in the mind, a sense of something taut, integral and *definitive*. As an illustration of what I mean, compare Michaels's 'The Second Search', presented as the lamentation of Marie Curie following the death of her husband, with MacLaine's 'Tending the Stone' in which the poet accompanies his mother to his father's grave and speaks vicariously through her sensibility. Whereas Michaels rests content with platitudinous elevations like 'The glowing distillation / of time' (meant obviously to allude to radium in a poem that is practically radioactive with it) or with a drowsy sententiousness like

> Everything we touch
> burns away, whether we give ourselves
> or not, the same April day spreads to thinness,
> the same winter afternoon
> thickens to dark. I was 38 years old.
> Every time a door opened
> I expected you. For months I hid your clothes
> stiff with blood ... ,

MacLaine works very close to the ground – a low-mower if ever there was one – prior to hewing out a series of peaty, concrete stanzas in which the poet tries to visualize and experience his mother's grief over the loss of her husband:

> I wonder what she thinks
> seeing that his dates are done,
> while hers, name and birth already cut,
> wait for time to finish its engraving.

She stands by
attending to the rightness of it all
while I shovel up last year's weeds,
tug out the rooty vetch,

shake loose the good soil from the sod,
fold in well-rotted sheep manure,
and stoop to throw a grub or two
well away beneath the one wild apple tree.

The difference I am trying to indicate here between the glow-worm flicker of a hopeful amateur and the steady, quiet luminosity of an accomplished talent becomes evident in their respective attempts at closure. Michaels trails off into a vague and predictable valediction which gropes in vain for the note of conclusive significance but merely ends up sounding phony and overdone, milking platitudes long gone dry:

I can only find you
by looking deeper; that's how love
leads us into the world.
My hands burn
all the time.

Looking deeper? That's how love leads us into the world? Yet more radium burning into the page? As any competent poet would see instantly, this is a poem stuck in draft mode, a mere sinopia waiting to be purged and worked up, scoured of clichés and easy, commodified feeling that betray its straining for effect. Compare the closing stanza of MacLaine's unpretentious meditation:

If nothing else, diggers in some later time
will see that here was one whose being
was not casual, and will conclude, I hope,
that someone found a meaning to a life.

*One whose being was not casual:* a poetic phrase that plugs into the memory socket as something bright, durable and *achieved.* Notice as well how the last line by the mere substitution of the preposition 'to' for 'of' and the insertion of the indefinite article before 'life' foxily skirts the 'meaning of life' cliché and ratchets the line up into a new realm of significance, hinting that meaning is always single and idiosyncratic and may with time, patience and labour be discovered by the end of a life or a poem. What the poem says by implication is that meaning cannot be imposed or fabricated if it is to abide and instruct. It must connect to the life and the work.

In trying to account for the difference between the two pieces, one might adapt another MacLaine line and propose that poems 'bloom according to the architecture of their soils,' and that the soils here (as elsewhere) are of different orders of fertility and vigour. With this distinction in mind and considering the way a good poem, regardless of how effortless it may sound, is never casual and always invests in the gradual discovery of an *integrated* meaning, let us return for a moment to another strand in the poetic fabric of (post)modern theory and practice that I touched on earlier. I refer to the tendency – and a rather unloving one at that – to break language down into its material constituents, syllable and breath, in order to strip away such distractions as meaning, clarity and communicative intent and to elutriate its principal nature, its pith and nucleus as body rather than as abstraction. An advanced contingent of Canadian poets, celebrating the profane loss of due notions and indulging in a kind of phthisic, unpersonable artistry, have embarked upon this striking linguistic adventure (cf. bill bissett, Paul Dutton and Fred Wah among many others, some of whom are given to shamanistic ululations in readings). I cite a brief section from Wah's 'Breathin' My Name with a Sigh', which reads like an unintentional take-off on Ben Jonson's 'Hymne to Cynthia' where the moonstruck poet-speaker petitions the 'Goddesse, excellently bright' to give the flying hart 'space to breathe, how short soever'. The Wah poem goes:

> Mmmmmmmm
> hm
> mmmmmmmm
> hm
> yuhh   Yeh   Yeh
> thuh moon

huh    wu    wu

nguh    nguh    nguh

w_____h

w_____h

Thuh pome huh wu dnt gv muuuch twirk wth in the anti-rhetorical impulse it expresses, as if it were taking seriously something like Robert Coover's *facetious* dismissal of 'the ungrateful diabolectical sesquipedalian' windbaggy tendency of language in his satirical extravaganza, *Pinocchio in Venice*. Nevertheless one may possibly detect the maverick purpose behind f_____d w_____h s reduction of language to its respiratory components, that is, to its foundational elements, presumably rehabilitating language to its nguhistic essence as breath and expletive, lung and solar plexus, in this palpitating prayer to the lunar goddess. Guud gawdd, wun mite respond, yuhh yuhh, a sendback if ever there wuz wun. Yet it duz gv usss sumthin to haww haawww about in a needlessly complicated and deceptive world predicated on the bulimic abuse of language. Sumthin to think about, too, hm hm wu wu Yeh.

Who knows? Perhaps all this has something to do with what appears to be our Alberta-based poets' obsession with breathing rather than with poetry, requiring a socio-ecological study of their habits and practices instead of a technical analysis of their verse. The proximity of the mountains could very well be a factor. Consider for example Doug Barbour's more recent emphysematous *breath ghazals* that go 'Aaahh' or 'ffmmm' or try to breathe 'efff' in vacuums of white space, poor things, expiring from the hiker's not the poet's customary altitude. As if this were not enough, '[I]magine the possibility of a held breath,' Barbour proposes, but before the reader asphyxiates in sympathy it is providentially exhaled in 'a shift / of attention    huh    here    & there.'

Others will disagree with my take on these pulmonary issues. For example, Judith Stamps in *Unthinking Modernity* links what I have carpeted here as a professional inanity with the restorative attempt to move from the sensory rigidities of a visual/spatial culture to a kind of oral/aural reading-and-writing practice that is said to recover the fluidity and dynamism of earlier pre-literate or more flexible manuscript cultures. Thus poets like the aforementioned bill bissett who court unintelligibility and are mainly conspicuous for lack of substance come in for considerable applause. But there is, I'm afraid, no going back. For we are the inheritors and scions of a nigh-millennial print culture, firmly embedded in its psychic plane of scansions and vectors, sensory ratios and temporal meridians, and cannot feasibly become a tribe of chanting enthusiasts who have chosen to have nothing to do with linear thinking and rational procedures, with orthography and syntax. These so-called innovations and virginal experiments with poetic language are really devastatingly archaic if not wholly obsolete. It is true that the retrieval of a fecund, dynamic and expressive sense of the word depends upon hearing – but hearing *internally* in the sound chambers of the inner ear where sonority *and* meaning cohere. And for this process of lexical redemption to occur we need, not heaps of raw syllables escorted by hyperventilation techniques, but words apt, nimble, svelte, resilient, laminar, spare, chatoyant, basilican, words simple and majestic, common and rare, words that regain their physicality because, like Lazarus, they come back to us as they once were, not decomposed into constituent bits and pieces but as integrated body rising once again in the living world of the imagination.

Nor, of course, should these words, or words as such, be conceived as mere abstract counters or nomothetic indicators, a tenet our 'sound poets' correctly hold but misapply as the basis for their congenial gim-mickry. The thesis that language is body before it is a law-dependent and cerebral network of abstract referents is shared by most serious poets and perceptive scholars and has, in fact, scarcely been challenged in our day. In Roman Jakobson's courtly formulation, 'The poetic function projects the principle of equivalence from the axis of selection into the axis of combination,' in other words, rhetorical paradigms, repetitions, parallelisms and phonetic symmetries (sounds, stresses, syllables) cut across the 'syntagmatic' continuity of the poem's conceptual syntax. This is the same principle that Samuel Levin writing in the early sixties called 'linguistic coupling' and Jacques Derrida at around the same time dubbed 'grammatology', asserting the priority of the signifier over the signified, i.e., that meaning is an effect of language, not a presence within or behind it, and that poetic articulation therefore occurs mainly at the level of the signifier: rhyme, rhythm, alliteration, assonance, ono-matopoeia, and so on. (For that matter, Edgar Allan Poe in *The*

*Philosophy of Composition* long ago identified this normal poetic practice as the 'principle of non-imitativeness'.) Similarly, to go back to roots and sources in the Homeric epics, epithets and similes are tucked into long stretches of recitation not for descriptive or expository but for *metrical* (and mnemonic) purposes. Thus, as has been often remarked, the storm god is not necessarily *nephelegerate Zeus* when he is gathering clouds but when he is filling out the staple double anapaest. This is why Achilles may be described as 'swift-footed' when he is sulking in his tent or sitting immobile talking to Priam.[6]

Poets (and the erudite scholiasts) have always known and / or applied this fundamental principle without having to engage in ludicrous disintegrations of language to prove what no real poet has ever interrogated or denied, that sound, euphony and morpheme are primary. The kind of degradation I am catechizing here has to do not so much with joining the *avant-garde* as with disconnecting from the athenaeum of received practices, either in mischief or ignorance. What I am disputing is the supposed validity of *toying* with self-evident axioms and especially with the basics of syllable and melody in so earnest and yet irresponsible a way, as if some irruption of bronchial truth or inspiration were shortly to issue from these ventral inquiries. But I hope it will be granted that I am not inveighing against the desire to experiment with the resources and possibilities of language and form, provided it is done both sensitively and sensibly, in a way that betokens knowledge of the long tradition, appropriateness to the subject and, crucially, an underlying intelligibility or accessibility. Parsing the chromatic and multiplex riches of the language he so palpably loves, here is Tim Lilburn in a poem called 'At the Center, A Woman', reviving an indigenous fable treating of the Creatrix as an instance of the 'Hymn to Proserpine'.

> Her voice is black water under wheat's erect earth.
> *Uh.   Uh.*
> Her teeth are armies.   *Uh.*
> Her throat's flex, tree, flowing mass. Cottonwood, beech.
> She sings the forest. Energy mezzos.
> *Mmho   Mmho   Mmho   Ho Ho Ho Ho*
> Horse, the great woman she holds the horse, the good, neck
>                     muscles of the turning horse.

She holds thigh bone, wing, herb, the stare of heron; her spine
                              is smoke, bones braided grass.
*Hooo   Hooo*
What she says, what she says, what
She says is the quack of a palm
Cupped under a squeezed armpit.
*Wa-hoo, wa.*
*Wa. Wa.*
*Hoo.*

This works. Lilburn, who has something of a religious and even mystical bent, is the real thing, a poet fully cognizant of his classical heritage, experimenting with rhythms and extended images much as his mentor Hopkins did, and intent on resurrecting through language, by dance and conjuration of a sprightly phonetics (and not without a certain bracing humour), the spirit of place his imagination – clothed round with the world's desire as with raiment – inhabits and elicits. The language stepping and swaying and capering in this poem is what Milton Acorn called 'Ojibway', words that express nature's thoughts, words, as Acorn put it, 'always steeped in memory', words that transform hope into action and come together at last to form Ojibway, 'which you can speak in any language'. Including Van Toorn's 'Wawa', the small Ontario town where the wind blows through people 'like a blues harp', or the 'hoos' of Stevens' portly Azcan.[7]

This may be the place to remind the reader that the poets I have upticked here as countervailing instances constitute the exceptions in a craft that has grown increasingly sceptical of apt words, memorable phrases, technical skill and, indeed, in Coleridge's dialect, of the work of the esemplastic imagination itself. Anne Carson's sudden emergence as a poetic eminence furnishes us with the most vivid contemporary example of how much of what was once considered essential has gone missing in today's poetic milieu. I will confine myself to a single example from the poetry, knowing that any other specimen would do as well in flaunting the absence of both memorable diction and audible music. In fact, her poetry reminds me of the sign you often see on Jettas and Accords to ward off thieves: *No Radio.* Though I suspect there never was a radio in the first place and the sign is just there for cachet. The piece I have chosen is called 'Methinks the Poor Town Has Been Troubled Too Long':

> Light on the brick wall and a north wind whipping the branches black.
> Shade draws the thread of the light out flat against its palm.
> Eat your soup, Mother, wherever you are in your mind.
> Winter noon is on the rise. Weak suns yet alive
> are as virtue to suns of that other day.
> For the poor town dreams
> of surrender, Mother
> never untender,
> Mother gallant
> and gay.

This standard issue Carson poem with its verbal triteness, rhythmic clunkiness and nascent sentimentality can only grate upon the sensibility of any reader not deluded by the hype that surrounds every new Carson production. What prosodic law can possibly govern this verse (a question, it is true, that can be asked of most contemporary work) apart from the purely mechanical brittleness and the cosmetic, typographical shrinking effect? The clichés just keep coming at you as if they had been computer-generated ('whipping the branches black', 'weak suns', dreams of surrender') and are even reinforced by alliteration ('gallant / and gay'). The limp rhyme meant to clinch the poem peters out in mere flapdoodle ('surrender, Mother / never untender') and the attempt at a kind of wistful music falters and expires as indeed is the case in almost every Carson poem. This lack of ear for cadence and accent and measure, this deadness to the *melos* at the heart of all complex structures, may represent her paramount failing as a poet. Carson could do worse than consult a text like Charles Butler's *The feminin' monarchi'* (c. 1634), which gives musical notes in triple time to represent the humming of bees when swarming and develops a madrigal set in four parts – mean, contratenor, tenor and bass – as an illustration of the primacy and binding quality of music as a universal principle of organization. What is true for the hive is true for the architecture of the poem, even the simplest lyrical artifact. But perhaps Carson is exempt from such desiderata if those who have called her a genius are right. I can't say exactly what the word signifies but it does prompt a reconsideration of Walter Bage-hot's observation: 'In the faculty of writing nonsense, stupidity is no match for genius.'[8]

To be fair, however, Carson is not appreciably worse than other decaf poets like Pimone Triplett – 'Love, love's no law of averages, and I bet / morning is no penny to be pinched back' – or Robyn Selman – 'Your mother worked … / Her ambition, she apologizes, / caused (like a virus?) awkwardness in the / kitchen' – or the droning and generic Robert Pinsky, that specialist of relationships, whose verse to my mind resembles his 'hoarse voice of Cookie, hawking / *The Daily Record* for thirty-five years.' There are certainly enough equally bad or even worse poets to go around to make the more conspicuously bad poets seem approximately toler-able, but this distributory fact does little to account for the exaltation of merely bad work at the expense of that slender modicum of exceptional writing with which we are still improbably blessed.

Contrast, for example, the above chunk of versified Carsonite with another poem about filial love and compassion, Michael Harris's 'Uncle Edward', whose title's avuncular displacement scarcely conceals the father he is memorializing. The poem is so accomplished in the flow and opulence of its language – the very antithesis of Carson's manneristic hiccuping – and so authoritative and assured in its sense of connection to that which comes before, its honouring of the *genuine* productive source which connects it to the reader's own experience, that it renders the unfolding of commentary almost unnecessary. Harris is in my esti-mation one of the finest lyrical talents we have. His voice, like Uncle Edward's, is the voice of a true poet, rising past 'the thinning insufficien-cies' of most current practice and culminating in 'the mortal heart and humour' of the real poetic afflatus, which the much put-upon reader has a right to demand or expect. There is no cheating, no self-election-eering, no wilful obscurity to be found here (or, for that matter, in any other Harris poem). The speaker, squinting through the keyhole at his father luxuriating in the bath ( his 'pink … tickled fully by water'), describes how, framed in 'the certainties of porcelain', each drip moves,

> like a fishing-bob, the winking pink of his penis.
> Outlandishly it peeks from the bulk of him
> at the love-songs and war-songs that wheel

circling each other above him; it eyes with awe
the patient polysyllables he herds like pods of whales
for a final sally through the Valley of the shadow.

Later, in bed, in a dry shroud of sheets,
he dreams a death at sea, watching his voice
rise up in bubbles past a parterre

of ungrateful urchins and bored whelks, past
a mezzanine's yawn of oysters, past a loge
stuffed with an awestruck, round-eyed gawk

of groupers, up through the roof of the sea,
past an exhausted mating codfish eaten whole
by a hungry shark; and with the bubbles expanding hugely

sail directly up to Heaven past the sun's
dying fire, past the thinning insufficiencies
of air, beyond the earth's wasting corpse

to burst in liquid glories, drowning
Heaven's whole angelic choir with
the mortal heart and humour of his song.

As we are on the subject of filiation (both personal and vocational), I should also cite at this juncture Eric Ormsby's beautiful homage to an aging mother. (As Norman Doidge deposed in *Books in Canada*, Ormsby is not simply 'one of the finest Canadian poets – but one of the handful of the best meditative poets writing in the English language'.) The signet of his talent is an eclectic fusion of precision and prodigality, of discipline and flamboyance, which we can detect in even so pensive and tranquil a poem as 'My Mother in Old Age', where the diminishment he laments is negotiated in perfections of diction and metaphor, not in the *trompe l'oeil* of easy typographical manipulations. The poem opens with a simple and vividly realized portrait-stroke:

As my mother ages and becomes
ever more fragile and precarious,
her hands dwindle under her rings
and the freckled skin at her throat
gathers in tender pleats like some startled fabric ...

and concludes in quiet amazement:

And yet she abets her metamorphosis,
invests herself in voluminous costume
jewels and shrill polyesters –
                              ambitious as a moth
            to mime the dangerous leaf on which she rests

– note the fragile 'moth' that shelters perilously in 'mother'. The effect we are left with is one of unabashed *sincerity*, which avoids both melodrama and effusiveness and does not inundate craft or strict technical control, as is generally the case with lesser writers for whom sincerity comes across as corny or maudlin. Consider in this regard another of Ormsby's poems on the same subject, entitled 'Childhood House', in which he once again pays tribute to the mother who shielded her children from 'the termite-nibbled floorboards and the rotting beams / ... the frayed, / unpredictable wiring ... / the fixtures in the dining room / skewed and malfunctioning,' bringing her into what we might call the elegiac present despite the fact that memory 'flits, occludes, is variable, sidesteps, bleeds away, eludes / all recovery' which would cause us to weep 'at the swiftness of that velocity / if our astonished eyes had time.' Yet the connection with the past is paradoxically maintained and recollection fixed in the face of the evanescence of all things, including memory, as a function of the poem exceeding its own reading, a perpetual pendulum of verbal events resisting dissipation or terminus. Preserving what he elsewhere calls 'a fragrance of time', there is a sense in which *the poem itself is memory*, opposing the very temporal annihilation it mourns.[9]

I would also like to draw attention in this context to Robyn Sarah's (note: not Robyn Selman's) lapidary sonnet 'On Closing the Apartment of My Grandparents of Blessed Memory', a masterful little elegy which lingers on in the memory with a poignancy owing directly to the poet's technical dexterity.

> And then I stood for the last time in that room.
> The key was in my hand. I held my ground,
> and listened to the quiet that was like a sound,
> and saw how the long sun of winter afternoon
> fell slantwise on the floorboards, making bloom
> the grain in the blond wood. (All they owned
> was once contained here.) At the window moaned
> a splinter of wind. I would be going soon.
>
> I would be going soon; but first I stood
> hearing the years turn in that emptied place
> whose fullness echoed. Whose familiar smell,
> of a tranquil life, lived simply, clung like a mood
> or a long-loved melody there. A lingering grace.
> Then I locked up, and rang the janitor's bell.

Sarah's work demonstrates how a commitment to the formal structures of poetry on the part of a talented poet helps to ensure its accessibility to the general reader as well as the preservation of sentiment from the scourge of sentimentality. When she is on her game, the poems dazzle like stellar circuitry. And it should be said that she is generally on her game. I know of few other poets on the national scene today who can make a sonnet, a villanelle or a sestina read like speech and yet adhere scrupulously to all the rules of construction and development. Sarah is a classicist by temperament who brings a formidable artistry to bear upon the realm of the domestic and the intimate, dignifying the commonplace by raising it to the level of paradigm.

Poets like Harris, Ormsby and Sarah, among the best we have, show us how it is possible to speak candidly, engage the reader directly and at the same time lace up a poem with consummate flair and assurance, using a lightly handled complexity of means to render and evoke the most intimate and powerful of human experiences, which are often the most resistant to articulation. The point is: the means are necessary to the effect.

When the means are conspicuously absent, the effect is doubly embarrassing, both for the poets who serenely display the penurious state of their equipment and for a lax and perfunctory audience that perseveres in lavishing doxologies upon them. A cardinal example of what I'm aiming at here may be found in the work of George Elliott Clarke. A target-rich area if ever there was one, his deficiencies as a poet incite a third embarrassment, namely, that of critical disclosure, for no decent person likes to rollick in another's unhappiness. But the callow disregard for the perplexity of human experience, the relentless launching of clichés like clay pigeons at a literary skeet-shoot, and the vapid self-satisfaction all too detectable in the permissiveness of loose diction and sockclock metaphor make Clarke, basking in newfound acclaim, one of the prime exhibits for the thesis I am developing. I reprint a passage from his anthologized 'Introduction to Modern Languages', in which he attempts to record the intimacy and grace of human love:

> The next October, your quick steps clattered
> over the narrow, cobbled streets of Québec,
> coming down to meet my train at midnight,
> *coming down to meet my train at midnight,*
> because my letters were much too lonely,
> their ink was tears you could see.

> You fried an omelette with ham and green pepper
> and jimmied red wine from the cramped fridge.
> The rain flared into snow because it had to –
> the temperature would not remain neutral.
> Leaves marshalled and assaulted the wind.
> We straggled through Québec…

And so on. I defy anyone to show me where the diction surges with power and delight, where the imagery arranges its pageantry, and where the music of these lines attunes the ear to harmonies of recognition, insight or even tenderness. Is the *italicized* repetition of 'coming down to meet my train at midnight' in any way incremental? Why is it there? The details assembled in a good poem are almost always purposeful and load-bearing but what do we gain from learning that the fridge is *cramped* or that the lady *jimmies* red wine from its shelves? And where is the logic in the leaves first marshalling and then treacherously assaulting the wind they have called or recruited, by connotative implication, as an ally? One hopes, at any rate, that the omelette fried with ham and green peppers redeemed the labour of composition, which on the evidence could not have been very exacting anyway.[10]

To see how this narrative approach to the poetic reproduction of quiet affection and communion is properly done, let us briefly consider a passage from Norm Sibum's 'Girls and Handsome Dogs', the title poem of his most recent book. The piece opens with the speaker engaged in a meditation on time, wondering as he strolls beneath its 'rosy cumulus' whether 'we are forever marching toward our capture / Or toward release,' observing rain falling on marigolds while temples slide into the sea, sketching runes in the sand, and pondering the 'comic shades / Of the absolute.' How to give shape and coherence to this incongruous collection of concepts and particulars becomes the question whose mark like the hook of curiosity draws the speaker forward toward the hope of diversion or maybe even companionship in a romantic encounter. But the poet realizes both the futility and the transient compensatory pleasure of his quest, realizes that

> To meet my addled heart I go, am in transit
> to an amorous spoor.
> By time's touch pushed along,
> My lazy progress
> Hastens. And even the flower in its box,
> A bird on its stalk, blooms
> With just the right hint
> Of concupiscence.
>
> Because all that eat
> Seek to exploit – by hand, by claw,
> by beak, by tooth –
> All that must eat know anxiousness.
> To love is to grow hungry and it is to banquet …

and agrees to settle, as he strolls on his way to his rendezvous between the copper domes of churches and the old on their constitutionals – the emblems of our condition – for the simple (and refreshingly *humorous*) anticipation of 'Delia's cucumber soup, Delia's passion for baroque strings'. ('O Delia, welcome me,' cries Tibullus to his mistress as he is borne toward her on Dawn's 'rosy horses', 'this is my only prayer'. See *Elegies*, I, iii. And likewise Samuel Daniel in his sonnets from *Delia*, knowing that beauty's 'short refresh ... cheers for a time.') Self-mockery predominates and the pride of the thinker, the metaphysician, the *vates*, the quester, the *flâneur*-poet who by reflection rises above the world he cannot subdue, is brought low as he prepares ironically to embark upon a humbler ascent, i.e., to 'rise up on my hind legs' and to 'beg for my portion.' A little food and a spot of romance – and perhaps the sweet of friendship – will have to do as an alternative to a satisfying epistemology or a mystical revelation. And the 'coupling' with tradition which the poem achieves secures the implicit sense of survivability that all genuine poems evince.

As a reader with his own natural hunger for real sustenance, I much prefer Sibum's cucumber soup to Clarke's fried omelette, for the fare Sibum provides covers the four spiritual food groups – humour, seriousness, discipline, humility – and is therefore wholesome and nutritive, not just a menu citation to fill out a line with improvident detail. The total absence of sentimentality in Sibum's poem; the saving grace of irony coupled with a sense of the *larger* past (not a merely personal or anecdotal one) inherent in the harking back to Augustine's meditation on time, the echo of Tibullus and Daniel, and the elliptical allusion to Shelley's Prince Athanase, 'Philosophy's accepted guest', who pities the tumult of our dark estate and owns no higher law than love; and the refusal to patronize the reader with coy obscurities, unsolicited confessions and portentous trivialities are the attributes that in a saner and less supercilious world would give Sibum the right to Clarke's audience.

And, *mutatis mutandis*, would give Ricardo Sternberg the right to Margaret Atwood's as well. These latter two poets share an unexpected proclivity for mapping the dark dimension of dreams, interior voyages and fluctuating relationships in terms of the *paysage moralisé*. But just as with Michaels and MacLaine, an initial perspectival and gestural affinity quickly drops out of sight. For Atwood suffers from what I am tempted to call the condition of spiritual rhinolalia, as evidenced by the priggish and anorexic appeal of her diction to an audience of poetic wannabes who require self-confirmation rather than aesthetic tournure or psychological truth. Tapping into the anxieties of the aspiring intellectual-poet, Atwood caters to the appetite for reduction in a proscenium of unsubstantiated desire.

Thus the connection with the reader is at bottom a fraudulent one, a form of mutual predation Atwood herself serendipitously describes in a poem called 'On the Streets, Love', in the figures of a billboard lady and a grey man. For the billboard lady and the grey man stand in as isomorphic substitutes for Margaret Atwood and her family of dependants, the satiety of the one depending on the voracity of the other, and vice versa. The middle passages read:

> (The billboard lady
> with her white enamel
> teeth and red
> enamel claws, is after

> > the men
> > when they pass her
> > never guess they have brought her
> > to life, or that her
> > body's made of cardboard, or in her
> > veins flows the drained
> > blood of their desire)

> (Look, the grey man
> his footsteps soft
> as flan-
> nel, glides from his poster

> > and the voracious women, seeing
> > him so trim,
> > edges clear as cut paper
> > eyes clean
> > and sharp as lettering,

want to own him

... are you dead? are you dead?

They say, hoping ... )

What we are witnessing is a perfect fit between the absence of talent in the writer and the absence of confidence in the reader, one lack subtending another, so that the symmetry that results is one of reciprocal idolatry. As far as I can see, there is no other way to account for the phenomenon of so limited, unsifted and monotonic a writer as Atwood being turned into a constellation.

When it comes to an encounter between Margaret Atwood and Ricardo Sternberg on the slopes of Mount Helicon, the latter has already signed the guestbook and left. In books like *The Invention of Honey* and *Map of Dreams*, Sternberg charts very much the same crepuscular territory as does Atwood in poems like 'Journey to the Interior' or 'A Night in the Royal Ontario Museum,' *et al.*, but does so with a verbal felicity and a haunting discant rhythm alert to divergences of mood and theme appropriate to the region he is exploring. Not that he cannot descend to the gruesome and graphic when the occasion requires it, but the force behind these poems is always that of blessing and wonder, a 'giving thanks / for the feast given him that day', a hymn to accompany the difficult alembicating journey toward 'soul-making' (Keats's word), which Sternberg depicts in the coda to *Map of Dreams* as 'journeys we must undertake / on the way back to ourselves.' Sternberg's poems do not cater to or merely reflect the empirical reader as do Atwood's but ask to be *boarded*, as it were, and travelled on toward necessary if elusive conclusions, so that what is activated in the reader is not the wish to be incorporated in the other but the need to transcend the given *with* the other, irrespective of the probability of failure and loss as foreseen by the captain of the ship in *Map of Dreams*:

*Though I hear nightingales,*
*smell the nectarines,*
*see honeycombs so laden*
*their gold overflows*

> *in a long, continuous tear,*
> *I fear I'll not set foot*
> *on that green shore.*

Even in the earlier *The Invention of Honey*, Sternberg distrusts the self as radically unfurnished and as self-deceiving, yet honours its longing for 'counter-love, original response' (Frost's words), the poet like a ragged scarecrow awaiting the reader in whose service he or she writes. Thus, in a lovely poem entitled 'Scarecrow', the sparrows and the farmer's wife, despite the distances they keep, are the conditions of the protagonist's authenticity and justify his solitary labour. And yet as an 'audience' for so dedicated a sentinel's performance of which they are the beneficiaries, they remain sadly absent. I cite the last three stanzas in which the scarecrow laments:

> My straw heart is almost gone.
> The wind moves through it
> with the hands of a ghost
> on an empty loom.
> It pleased me when the sparrows
> would pluck the heartstuff
> and build their nests from it.
> I felt then as if I flew.
> But they have kept away.
>
> I have wished for love
> from the farmer's wife.
> In my dreams she would come
> to take from the threadbare heart
> one more straw
> and chew slowly on its sweetness,
> looking out from the darkened field,
> flying from far away into herself.
> She too has kept away.
>
> I will not be here
> next year to bless the corn.

The melancholy of the piece is further deepened and extended by its reminiscence of Richard Wilbur's well-known 'Sonnet' (in which an abandoned scarecrow, with its 'gestures of invincible desire', braves the heart-eclipsing night 'div[ing] down like one great crow') as well as of Buson's moving haiku:

> Owner of the field
> goes to see how his scarecrow is,
> comes back.

The scarecrow, however, whose love, soul and speech go unreciprocated by both a proprietary audience and an aviary of winged specialists, does not come back. The irony, of course, is that Ricardo Sternberg, as our poet of soul-making and counter-love, lives and writes in a literary milieu which fore-grounds neither. And as for original response, passing over for the moment the rare poets I am trying in these pages to bring to the reader's attention since they too may not come back, it plainly does not reverberate very far either.

Let us compare the work of two more poets. One I hope will return often; the other I suspect will shortly and deservedly fade away as merely another flavour of the month. Mary Dalton is a Newfoundland poet who has mined the 'ripply' dialect (to use her own adjective), the idioms and rhythms of her native region to give us a rousing and spirited verse that 'marley[s] back' to us with its brimful berry pails (see 'Berry Pails') or behaves like the wind she writes about in 'Conkerbells',

> barreling out of the north
> Canvas lifting up off the floor
> And conkerbells hanging thicker than
> A horse's dong,

a poetry like her own dogger who

> tripped in the juniper
> Toppled arse-over-teakettle
> Smack into the boughs of our hot little tilt.

Dalton has produced only two books to date and has just completed a third but the work gives ample evidence of a steadily growing talent able to tackle the accents and timbres of parochial speech and raise them to the power of poetry. This is by no means an easy task as most poets who attempt so subtle a metamorphosis generally remain gridlocked in the prosaic and hackneyed registers, either because their range of selection is poor or their phrasing is inadequate. In Dalton's case, however, the novel blend of lilt, brogue and aphorism produces a signature diction. The sense of kinship to a salty and invigorating language, a kind of love match between imagination and word that transcends the regionality of its source and creates a new and nonlocalized world whose coordinates become the reader's, enhances our own relationship to the commonplace – in the same way, as Andrew Wainwright says in his biography of Charles Bruce, that 'the language of his region provided sound and sense for any part of the country.' It redeems everydayness in a way that is lasting, sharpening our awareness of our own speech rhythms and the sheer pleasure of an articulation in which the useful finds room for the joyfully excessive, so it need not 'turn sour as a witch's tit' or shrink from enjoying 'a racket with the weather'.

By contrast, Christian Bök's thesaurus-driven wordplay in his extended lipogram *Eunoia* (dedicated 'for the new ennui in you') gives evidence only of a conjuror's tricksy expertise, leaving no abiding impression except that of encapsulated dexterity and a valedictory question: *Why would anyone want to do this?* If it survives, it will do so merely as a curiosity, like a page of the phone book inscribed on a postage stamp. Passages such as

> we vow
> solo love
>
> we see
> love solve loss
>
> else we see
> love sow woe

selves we woo
we lose

lay out the problem with unintentional precision. The cosseted poetic self does indeed tend to get lost, considering that our poet, like his Ubu (but unlike Jarry's), 'blurts untruth: much bunkum (plus bull), much humbug (plus bunk)'. The 'verse paragraphs' he traffics in, each hi-liting a single vowel to the exclusion of the other four, are funky and ingenious in an algorithmic sort of way, showing what can be done when one puts one's mind to one or another form of Trivial Pursuit. But they are nevertheless mere lipid vesicles or word-sacs that might one day have been synthesized by a serious mind into something more complex and meaningful. As poems, they are resolutely nonpuerperal – though he calls the book a 'consummation' – and do not offer to connect with the demands and contingencies of human experience. The univocalic play with language, while skilful and adroit, leads absolutely nowhere and dissolves in mere entertainment whose pleasure is over once the performance is done or the game finished. (Far more fun, if that is what one is looking for, is Paul-Marie Lapointe's Oulipian and Joycean tour de force, *Le Sacre*, a gigantic expansion of French-Canada's idiomatic blasphemy, *tabernac*.) And the fact that Bök is practising a literary diversion harking back to the earlier part of the twentieth century and long ago exhausted by the European avant-garde only adds to the absurdity of the project, which is about as with-it as reinventing the Catherine wheel. The ennui is not so new. At best, *Eunoia* would make an interesting children's book – the new Mother Goose or Dr. Seuss – if it were suitably abridged and came with pictures.

The difference between the work of Dalton and Bök is the difference between language that releases the energies of communication (in which use accommodates surplus) and language that calls attention only to its own exorbitance (in which lack becomes a form of superfluity), or say, between the real tonality of honest and substantial expression and sham umlauts à la Häagen-Dazs.[11] (Umlaut's ubiquity ultrafies unction.) Timothy Steele is surely right when he argues that *all the fun's in how you say a thing* – the title of his recent book on prosody – but the implicit provision of his thesis is that there needs to be a *thing* there in the first place to be said, and that the saying involves metre, versification, rhythmical modulations and cadence in general, not pointless and arbitrary rules of exclusion manipulated with typical Oulipostor facility. All we are getting, whatever way we want to look at it, is the poetry of disavowal. The next step our prodigies of restriction might contemplate, which one may be pardoned for looking forward to, would be to produce a book of poems in which *all* the letters of the alphabet were eliminated.

I will conclude this portion of my argument with a last set of matching incompatibles, always keeping to the hymeneal and/or genealogical mode of intimacy, relation, affinity and correspondence to accord with my overall theme. When we read the dishevelled and anaemic stanzas of Michael Ondaatje's 'Rock Bottom' (of which I give a short but representative section), a poem that differs from its typical confederates only insofar as it manages to combine speech and prose into a single undistinguished idiolect, we might find ourselves inclined to agree with the 'message' with which the poem, in its manifest lack of complexity and its technical rudimentariness, fatally consorts.

> We grow less complex
> We reduce ourselves    The way lovers
> have their small cheap charms
> silver lizard,
> a stone
>
> Ancient customs
> that grow from dust
>                    swirled out
> from prairie into tropic
>
> Strange how the odours meet
> How, however briefly, bedraggled
> history
>        focusses

What is Ondaatje actually *saying* here? Does not the apparent simplicity of the piece disguise a fundamental obscurity of meaning or intention and a pretentiousness of implication? Can one *really imagine* the lovers with their lizards and stones, which have been dragged into the poem as an emblem of diminishment? And is not whatever underlying theme or purpose we may discern further bedimmed by the unmotivated stanza breaks, the inconsistent punctuation, the enigmatic line indentations, the phonetic awkwardness ('*how, how*ever'), the humdrum diction ('swirled out', 'bedraggled history'), the grammatical discrepancy (why no indefinite article before 'silver lizard' if 'stone' requires one in the enumeration?), in short, by the technical ineptitude of the piece in general, so that the title becomes undesignedly apposite?[12] And yet Ondaatje is an internationally celebrated writer, not only as a novelist but as one of the cinematic *Sons of Captain Poetry*, who, we might think, should know and do better than to give us poems with the Tyvek still showing.

I would argue that Ondaatje, no less than poets like Purdy and Snyder and Creeley and Ashbery and Carson and a thronging host of others, whether they materialize as plebs or cabbalists, are an expression of a cultural syndrome I have elsewhere proposed calling 'the Missing Emperor', which is to say: it is not that the emperor has no clothes but that there is no emperor there in the first place to suffer the embarrassment of vestimentary disclosure. There is only an eidolon, an illusion of a writer, an intellectual dybbuk, an emanation, a virtual Idoru, an embodied rumour, a conventional effect, or in a phrase, a collective figment that comes into constative existence because a certain sector of the effective community has decreed it and a credulous or sectarian, designated public has believed it.

In politics, this is the same dynamic that could take a telegenic nonentity with a somewhat dazed expression and turn him into the head of the Canadian Alliance. In literature, it is a dynamic that has raised inadequacy and lack to the status of an accomplishment requiring public recognition. This explains why, for example, E. D. Blodgett – whose poems, as Carmine Starnino has shown in an article in *Canadian Notes & Queries*, may be written backward without the reader noticing much difference – can garner a Governor General's Award, and Margaret Atwood – whom columnist Pierre Foglia of the Montreal French language daily *La Presse* calls '*la soporifique prima donna de la littérature canadienne*' – can receive a Booker Prize on the fourth attempt, to reward her for having failed on the previous three.

It is almost as if the substance and quality of the work no longer matter in a context dominated by mere superfluities and accidents like name, precedence, influence, image and especially persona; as if our hearts were no longer capable of being stirred by 'the achieve of, the mastery of the thing' that emerges from the discipline and splendour of imaginative honesty and craft proficiency; as if, in fact, scrupulous aesthetic judgement had now become synonymous with courage in an age of timorous and unfoundable commitments. But courage is in short supply these days, as are common sense and a willingness to trust one's own educated instincts before the deflections and blandishments of a purely spectacle culture, a culture growing progressively disconnected from its origins and tellingly indifferent to the preservation of the skill traditions, that is, a culture becoming increasingly *unreal*. Thus, for the most part, literary discourse has succumbed to the toxins of that false and minimal predication associated with something like the Academy Awards – in at least two specifications of the term.

Let us go back to the Ondaatje poem once more and contrast that insubstantial exercise-in-disconnection-from-any-possible-sustaining-medium (be it love or history) with what is literally a manifest *achievement*: the bountifully physical, Anglo-Saxon, staple four-beat measure, the brisk and lively diction and the sensual imagery of Rodney Jones's 'On Censorship', a poem about love and connection and language and finding and being found, the central themes of this polemic. The poem begins:

> It is not going to disturb anything in the least
> If I say to the brown wren that the bumblebee,
> Who just a minute ago thundered by here like a bull
> Whumping against the table legs and the trunks of saplings,
> Has gone and insinuated himself deep
> In the spiraling black lace of the blackberry vine
> And right now is sneaking a little poontang
> Among the tender yellow labia of the buttercups ...

One thinks of the other Jones, country-and-western singer George, who warbles about being catapulted 'smack dab into the middle of love'. But in the poem, of course, the verbal ante is sharply raised. '[P]oontang,' like Van Toorn's 'balling' and 'humping' but unlike Purdy's 'boing[ing],' works marvellously in the diversified economy of the piece, for the humour is subsumed in the sumptuous language and kinetic rhythms and need not call undue attention to itself like a single crop on which too much is made to depend. On the contrary, these are poems that, like Jones's grandmother's biscuits in 'Bread', 'ha[ve] the entire farm in them' and whose excellence remains a constant in the table's 'Macaronian variations', poems whose making is like the rising of that matriarch's loaves, 'the whole / house priming with the ale essence of yeast'. And where, as well, there may be found between the poet and the reader (as in a similar way between the grandson and the grandmother in Jones's poem) a kind of miscible chemistry based on artisanal respect and open trust, a mutual appreciation of the craftsmanship involved in both writing and reading well – or, if one likes, the compact of anticipated excellence. For these are poems erected at the intersection between the desiring poet, the ancestors and incunabula the poet reveres, and, perhaps most important, the projected intimacy binding the real poet and the imagined 'common reader', thus invoking two important audiences typically disregarded by most contemporary poets. This imagined reader especially, without whose collaboration the poem tends to become an exercise in fatuity or abstruseness, is the same reader, 'unnoticed by the monocled eye of History', whom Billy Collins summons in the poem that introduces *The Art of Drowning*, entitled 'Dear Reader'. This is the reader the poet recognizes as the 'dark silent figure standing / in the doorway of these words' and who could just as well be 'the man I held the door for / this morning at the bank or post office' or 'the face behind the wheel of an oncoming car' on the 'road we can't help travelling together'.

# 3.

I REALIZE THAT THESE REMONSTRANCES of mine may sound as if I am trying to revive the obsolete notion of poetic diction, as first articulated by John Dennis who commented on 'the differences between a Poetick and a Prosaic diction', and taken up next by Pope when he wrote of Homer that 'we acknowledge him the Father of Poetical diction, the first who taught that Language of the Gods to Men.' But the theory of poetic diction as it evolved in the eighteenth century is not as rigid and elementary as it may seem at first blush, since it came in at least two colours: (1) that certain words are specifically suited for poetry, a position defended by Thomas Gray who claimed that poetry should possess 'a language peculiar to itself'; and (2) that some words, either because they are too common or too obscure, are not suitable for poetry at all.[13]

My protest against the flat and anhedonic diction favoured by most contemporary poets obviously derives in part from the second formulation, although I am also conscious of the persuasiveness of Mayakovsky's assertion, amplifying a passage in Rilke, that when a word enters a poem, it thereby becomes a poetic word or epithet and is consequently self-justified and inviolable. (His example is 'Great Bear'.) Similarly Paul Celan adverts to 'the How and Why of that qualitative change the word experiences, to become a word in a poem ... ' The converse of these affirmations would then hold as well: if, as Sidney writes in *The Defence of Poesy*, even one word is lost from a poem, 'the whole work fails, every word having his natural seat, which seat must needs make the word remembered'. My own feeling is that a flexible and judicious appreciation of poetic language has its source in the conceptual middle ground between formulation (2) and Rilke/Mayakovsky/Celan/Sidney. Another way of looking at the question is to regard the creation of a viable poetic language as the struggle to attain a workable mix of common and aureate words, as Yeats advocated when in a late poem he congratulated himself with his disarming brand of aristocratic concession for having acquired 'Grounds where plum and cabbage grew'. Ditto for Wallace Stevens who, coming at the matter from the cabbage side (though with brassican esprit) in 'Notes Toward a Supreme Fiction', advised the poet to 'compound the imagination's Latin with / the lingua franca et jocundissima' and thus devise a language with roots in both the grapholect and the common koine.

In any case, what I am concerned with here is not prescribing *ex cathedra* the rules and principles of poetic diction or recycling some hoary *Gradus ad Parnassum* or lobbying for *ye distant spires, ye antique towers*, but with making a brief for the distinctiveness of poetic language as something substantively different in its nature from the everyday use of language, even if we posit the vocabulary of the former as coextensive with that of the latter – which in some instances may still lead to the kind of difficulties I have sketched. What I want to do is draw the reader's attention to those poems, where they can be found, that are so verbally rich and juicy they are like peaches you have to take your shirt off to eat, as opposed to the withered and desiccated nubbins of verse we are usually proffered for our malnourishment. It is really a question of how we approach the lexicon: whether it is lovingly cultivated over time or simply plundered off the bush, dexterously pruned or merely lopped. In the latter event, the result is sometimes happy, but more often inconsistent and most often unimpressive.

For everyday informal talk is by nature haphazard, not always responsible, structurally loose, and replete with irrelevancies, gaps, phatics, pauses, fillers and mini-audibles. Poetic expression is, in the case of *every one* of these traits of workaday impromptu talk, the complete antithesis – unless that given feature is deliberately staged, as in the Sharon Olds poem. Poetry, as a *transformation* of concrete everyday talk, enjoys a totally different realm status. In other words, a poem is always in other words. Poets who compose or extol work which purportedly resembles everyday speech betray a crippling misunderstanding of their craft and run the danger of conflating the literal with the literary.[14] Whatever way we want to look at the finished product, there can be nothing aleatory or 'conversational' about it. Rather, the scripted play of words, cadences and ideas bracketed within the poetic frame is basically both ritualistic and after-the-fact, the poet working with a set of specific rules and determinate resources to maximize the chances that come her or his way, moving ineluctably toward a consistent, always replayable or revisable (thus retrospectively controlled) and hopefully fortunate outcome. Poetic language works by a process of 'iconolexis' so that meaning and function coalesce and words do or resemble what they say, originating novelty in and by means of the very act of *manifesting* what we may already know. But the *actual* rhythms and gradients of 'common speech' – which are, in David Bohm's term, constitutively 'irre-factant' since spoken words, accompanied by gesture and intonation, need not fit the performative context by reproducing content on their own[15] – remain innately foreign to poetic composition, although the vocabulary of the former is restrictively admissible into the latter.[16]

To put it another way, the words that poetry uses come from the communal fund of language it shares with prose and speech, but the lexical filter it applies and the *way* in which it uses the words it assimilates and organizes, the rhythms, etymons, symbolic transforms, objective patternings and layered or subliminal connotations it deploys, are uniquely its own. The poet should never forfeit the pleasure of the page lenticulated with seemly or prismatic words that yield to the reader through both phrasal and formal means the sense of fulfilment a discernible or intuited meaning confers under befitting prosodic circumstances. This is what enables a poem to survive its occasion. Its precision, its verbal biconvexity and its sensed valence of higher import – its aura – are what make a poem answerable to the world and something other than a snippet, a transcript, a mere rumination, a record of the speaking voice or a log of one's *personal* proclivities and *private* experiences, one's individual sufferings and ecstasies, as if intimacy were a condition of currency. (How liberating it would be, as Robert Hass says in *Twentieth Century Pleasures*, 'to read a poetry by people who did not assume that the great drama in their work was that everything in the world was happening to them for the first time.') One thing remains incontestable. No matter how ostensibly unpremeditated or improvised or nakedly confessional or fragmented or mundane it may *appear*, poetic language must remain *intrinsically* formal and hieratic if it is not to dissipate in mere gush or wind, mere divulgence of self.[17] Or, alternatively, if it is not to coagulate in the viscid incomprehensibility associated with what I have called the vatic branch of the neobardic enterprise, where the impetus is toward a more recondite and inaccessible phrasing although the language remains equally vapid. Bavius or Maevius, same difference.[18]

Poetry, then, is *artificial*. 'What makes the writing of even good prose so difficult,' reasons Paul Fussell, 'is that its conventions of logic, coherence, emphasis and economy are so unnatural to us. [Thus] we can sense the infinitely larger world of artificiality in which a poet works.' Further, it is in the very artificiality of the poetic artifact, in the structure of grace rather than that of nature, that poetic power is both contained and generated. As Richard Wilbur affirms in 'Ceremony', a homage to his severe yet sportive Muse (based on the pivotal figure in Frédéric Bazille's painting, *Réunion de famille,* which now hangs in the Musée d'Orsay), whom the poet opposes to Milton's anodyne Sabrina, goddess of the river Severn, from *Comus:*

> What's lightly hid is deepest understood,
> And when with social smile and formal dress
> She teaches leaves to curtsey and quadrille,
> I think there are most tigers in the wood.

It is this seemingly paradoxical quality of formal constraint marching along with verbal *sprezzatura* and delight – what Virgil in the *Eclogues* described as brambles bearing spikenard – that produces the breaker of creative force animating the poetic construct and gives us poems distinguished not only by the wham colours of their rhetoric or the subtlety of their implications but by the ability to carry a semantic expansion to many decimal places. These are poems with multiple impact, formal, lexical and expressive, precisely because of that condign mix of contraries, the protean and the austere. Formulation (1) above – that poetry must shop at an exclusive boutique for its verbal wardrobe – plainly does not merit extensive consideration, but on the other hand too much Great Bear can devour the freshness, texture, nuance and density of a poem as well.

The genuine poet, I am further suggesting, loves not only the actual language in which he or she revels and exults but also the potential reader who is in some ways as close as a sexual partner, the one in congress with whom the poet conceives meaning, creates beauty and generates a progeny of intimate and lasting effects in poems – as Harry

Bailey says in the Prologue to *The Canterbury Tales* – of 'best sentence and moost solaas.' But when language slumps into the unreconstructed vernacular or curdles into the sham oracular, or both, when the vapourings of friendly critics are treated by the faithful as infallible verdicts, and when the reader is *by necessity* one's own confederate and accomplice (given that these poets have purposively disconnected from a veridical readership) the result is woefully predictable, a debased product of approved literary sentiment whose only interest or appeal is to a small party of aficionados.

It is also true that the layperson is at present equally oblivious to the sporadic remnant of admirable poets in our midst. This is a fact we have no alternative but to accept while hoping it may one day change. But my point is that it is usually the pedestrian or entrepreneurial crew who make a great fuss about the social – and sometimes metaphysical – value of their production.[19] At a certain moment in the lives of these poets a bad decision was taken – the decision to write in one of the two related modes described earlier, to hitch their wagon not to a star but to bits of floating debris or tiny asteroids, to adopt the specious mythology of an etiological lineage intended to consecrate a national psyche, and to devise new experiments in form which, as Russell Smith has testified in a *Globe and Mail* column, result in 'exciting the experts while alienating the readers.' But even the hippest poetry has somehow to grandfather its source in the history of the craft, paying obeisance to its origins at the same time as it strives to break new ground, if it wishes to be taken seriously. Otherwise it merely floats in a temporal void, relying on spectacle to make itself felt rather than on what Friedrich Schiller in his *Athenaeum Fragments*, drawing from numismatics, called 'noble rust': 'The art of counterfeiting has managed to imitate everything except this minting of time. There's also a noble rust on people, heroes, philosophers, poets.'

Thus the latest 'performance' trends clamouring for our attention: that frenzied and self-promoting balderdash called Fusion Poetry self-described as crossing the boundaries between 'spoken word, Gen X, web-page poems, slam and MTV-style telepoetics,' but affording material only for mortified recantation once its exponents reach adulthood. The cluck and gabble of something like Toronto poet Paul Vermeersch's *The IV Lounge Reader* and the 'school' it represents is only marginally less preposterous. A similar injunction would apply to the recent publication of an 'oral' history of the performance scene in Montreal, entitled *Impure*, which spotlights the thoughts, habits and exploits of this new class of troubadours happily working in a language that is not working in them. And perhaps least interesting of all is another Montreal attempt to keep up with literary fashion, the women's collective called Ribsauce, which purports to investigate 'the intersections between text and performance, language and sound-places' and to garnish our plates with 'tang-tasty, irreverent new work from the new generation of Canadian women writers' – who despite the repeated emphasis on newness seem to be lagging about a generation behind Gertrude Stein. (All these forms of 'spoken word' poetry should be seen for what they are: the lower rap.) Each of these moves and movements is the inescapable result of that prior, axial bad decision.[20] Noble rust will not accumulate here. And yet that bad decision was probably inevitable, for one may perhaps simplify a little and say, *tout court:* good poets don't make bad decisions. The wand chooses the wizard.

Odd as it may sound, I don't wish to suggest that bad poets are necessarily untalented. But the fact is that there are talented people everywhere in the world. Some can balance broomsticks on their noses, others can do wonders with a skateboard, still others can perform univocalic capers, excel at plodding marathons or declaim nonsense with animation at poetry slams. But I am saying that the good poets, unlike the crowd of mountebanks in which they are in danger of disappearing, tend to concentrate on the *work* itself, where it shows, like Christopher Smart's Jeoffry, in electrical fire, spiritual substance and the ability to tread all the measures upon the music. Labouring in defiance of the aesthetic and political orthodoxies of the times, the latter are the exceptions who may one day, with luck and despite unlikelihood, look forward to a small but receptive lay audience for their work, powering on past the dabblers and poseurs, the coteries and the experimental farms, making it where everyone else failed to make it and doing it, whatever the consequences, *allegro con brio.* And this is because the poem as shapely utterance, as a *constructed linguistic object irradiated by lexical joy no matter what its subject,* and as something both demanding and accessible is precisely what the potential, nonspecialist and sympathetic reader who forms the poet's ideal audience expects and deserves.

It stands to reason that a good poem needs to be richly oxygenated with purpose, which makes itself felt in idea, language and metaphor. The same sense of urgency adheres to the integrity of formal structure, whether present or implied, since the predisposition toward form should not be regarded as a timid mollification of the preterite but as an antidote to the dispersions of undigested experience, the brangle of surds, free-floating data and unshaped givens of which daily life consists. In addition – to reiterate – we must also establish a syzygial connection with a possible reader rather than become what that weathered infanta of the Québécoise scene Nicole Brossard has cried up in her *Installations* as 'a holographic body spiralling into space' – or, for that matter, the invisible body of Jenny Boully's stunt-like concept book *The Body* walking on footnotes. The poet's business is to write poems that build up a kind of inner equity for their readers and contribute to their intellectual and emotional solvency. As I have suggested throughout, the poet should treat the reader with the tenderness and respect with which one approaches another person whom one happens to love or, at the very least, feels a certain responsibility toward. There is always an exchange of courtesies involved, a double flow of sympathy and concern. Charles Simic gets it right in an occasional stanza written for *The Paris Review*'s 'Reflections on a Worksheet' section (Number 154) where he is discussing Byron's *Don Juan*:

> The poet and the reader gaze upon each other
> With swimming looks of speechless tenderness
> Which mix'd all feelings, friend, child, lover, brother;
> All that the words can hide and express
> When two pure hearts are pour'd in one another,
> And love too much, and yet cannot love less ... [21]

Regrettably, the situation is now that on the long spectrum between risk and compromise, audacity and preconcertedness, seductive hazard and a kind of fashionable, tame, formulated 'novelty', between yeoman execution in a resistant medium and a prosody of cosmetic touch-ups of ordinary speech, we have moved alarmingly toward the latter pole – thus alienating the intelligent lay reader. (The epigraph from Roberta Rees makes it painfully obvious where our poetry has gone wrong.)

Perhaps this situation will change one day and, as Elise Partridge – one of the very few poets of value currently writing on the west coast – suggests in a poem called 'Inspiration', we may dream a prevailing wind that 'shakes loose a scatter of gold'. Perhaps the pack of tireless incompetents who club together and clutter the scene will be duly checked – a fate no doubt highly improbable but richly deserved, like a golfer being struck by lightning.[22] The trouble is that as things stand today, our poets on the whole no longer require a genuine audience, no matter how small, as a condition of survival or legitimacy. They require only an influential group of poetic, corporate and institutional patrons along with a camera crew. As Michael Schmidt remarked in a PNR editorial, the culture of reception is no longer consistently serious. 'Nowadays, a very few poets are ceremonially received, and the reception is wine and crisps, pious speeches and a cheque ... The media are there to report the news: prizes are news, poetry isn't. There is no space for readerly engagement, questions of accountability don't arise.'

Thus, adept in the art of gaming the system, it is the lek of self-proclaimed poets itself, what Pope called 'the club of Quidnuncs', now much expanded, along with the satellite networks of promoters, commentators and logothetes, who keep one another merrily boinging along, complaisantly blind to questions of merit, discipline, gist and craftsmanship. For without the *incorporate monologue* that unites this literary consortium, like the blended voice of the Borg which Captain Picard continues to hear and resist, they would have nothing left to write but their obituaries.

# Conclusion

THE PREDICAMENT I HAVE BEEN CONFRONTING is a pervasive one with parallels in many other fields and disciplines, most notably law and architecture, but applying no doubt to cultural life in general. As William Hubbard writes in *Complicity and Conviction: Steps toward an Architecture of Convention*, we want our constructs – poems, statutes, buildings – 'to embody qualities more enduring than those of the moment, yet we want them to speak to us in forms that have meaning right now.' Ideally, he suggests, we strive to accomplish or accommodate work that reflects change in the present yet gives an impression of continuity and stability. This antinomy is central to dynamic and evolutionary cultures and generates the tension that provides for genuine novelty and difference. In those instances when one or another of the poles of the dilemma is cancelled, stagnation befalls. In the current scenario, it is the pole of continuity that has been discredited as an oppression or obstacle to 'progress.' In such cases what may appear progressive, new, brave, original, adventurous – think of Marinetti and the Futurists – is really a retrograde and self-indulgent expression of infantile stasis-in-the-moment dissembled as a reverie of the future.

Hubbard examines many different occupations and disciplines apart from those mentioned above, including typography and games. Of the latter he writes most interestingly, 'We know how, in a game, we might be tempted to succumb to a momentary desire but, if we want truly to play the game for the sake of experiencing the play, then we are actually grateful that the rule is there, forcing us to hold to our ideals. The rules check the tendencies in ourselves that we consider unworthy and free the tendencies we consider ideal.' He continues with a discussion of law. 'The law too embodies this kind of wisdom about human nature. When the law works as it should, it holds us to the things we consider enduring and ideal and keeps us from doing the things we consider momentary.' I submit that there is also a 'law' of poetic creativity which holds us to the things we consider enduring and ideal and keeps us from doing the things we consider momentary, but unfortunately it is a law now increasingly disregarded.

In the arts as well as in the culture at large, this seems to be the false and asyndetic position in which we now find ourselves. Rejecting what Orlando in *As You Like It* calls 'the constant service of the antique world', we seem to have forgotten that the past, while it resembles the present insofar as it is equally compounded of ignorance and atrocity, is also the enduring and productive ground 'against' which – in both senses of the term – the figure of the present takes on shape, coherence and meaning. In legal terms, the past is *stare decisis*, a given, which determines licit behaviour but also allows for departures by providing a measure or benchmark from which to take our bearings and bring in modifications. For principles of conduct and construction in any cultural domain cannot be invented merely for the occasion or adopted with a kind of neoteric insouciance unless we accept that they can be instantly jettisoned as well in the interests of something 'new' or unforeseen, leading to a crisis of dereliction. Poetically, the result of this practice of constantly renovated virginity would be nothing less or more than anarchy, a disconnection in the two dimensions of tradition and readership, so that the best its proponents might hope for in the long run or legitimately implore is the passing tribute of a sigh.

In the best poetry, the past is represented by continuity of general theme – Yeats once said that only two things can interest a serious mind, sex and the dead, and he was not far wrong – and by the persistence of structural templates whose long pedigree strongly implies their adequacy to the general forms of human experience and, as I have maintained, their recombinant adaptability to account for the unprecedented.[23] Naturally, as indicated at the outset, the issue of aesthetic judgement is notoriously cloudy and insecure, but this misfortune does not absolve us – in whatever aesthetic, literary or critical camp we situate ourselves – from the obligation to sift, weigh and assess, and to render judgement as honestly and stringently as we can. I have plainly flailed about me with considerable abandon and have spared neither the striking where I thought necessary nor the stroking where I thought deserving. But I have tried to base my judgements on a set of criteria, enumerated in endnote 3, which are reasonably distinct, unequivocal and perdurable. In doing so I hope it will be accepted that I am not plumping for a return to an antediluvian rhetoric like some sort of latter-day Langland starting a *Piers Plowman* campaign to bring back alliterative verse, as if the Norman conquest (or the twentieth century) had never happened. The criteria I invoke are perennial to poetry and not just a swatch of antiquated presuppositions and principles as some may allege. On a more subjective level, perhaps, I have argued that what makes a poem memorable and worthy of consultation is in large measure a concern with language far more than a preoccupation with emotion. Language abides, but emotion tends to evaporate and is indeed often bogus and trivial – and what is more, can be preserved only in fit and vivacious words. Of course, the 'language' I am speaking of is language that is worked and polished, not the volatile and utilitarian counters of everyday speech and functional prose. It is what the strong poet David Barber refers to in a verbally munificent piece called 'The Threshers' as the implements of the world coming down to us 'in the garb of a verb', as language whipped like 'ripe wheat' into shape 'by mulling it over, working it through, thrashing it out'.

What I have called standard practice is, in light of the above, defective, mediocre and trifling, if not for the most part entirely negligible. Yet these poems, at best merely early instars of a deferred consummation, command our selective attention owing to the promotional monopoly of literary affairs concentrated in the hands of an influential sodality of critics, reviewers, chalky academics, granting officers and of the various leagues and cliques in which poets combine to exercise authority and, so to speak, corner markets. 'It is important and necessary,' remarks Joan Houlihan in an on-line article in the *Boston Comment*, 'to reject the notion that a poet, renowned or not, can perpetrate this continuing fraud of passing off their [sic] amateurish or unfinished prose jottings as poems,' and goes on to lay the blame with 'the machinery of publication' staffed with friendly, ignorant or irresponsible editors.

As a consequence these 'to-do lists and mind doodles' pretending to be poems heave into public view and consciousness – to the limited extent that they do – garnering disproportionate and unmerited attention, accompanied at times by some quite astounding emoluments. The merdiness of this work survives only in virtue of a kind of analogical certification: i.e., the thing looks like a poem, a validating tradition continues to be vaguely intuited in the mind of 'the public', and in certain cases the celebrity of the poet transfers spuriously to the viability of the artifact, thus conferring an importance to which the object has no claim. But I would like to believe that something like the Pribislav Hippe Effect will eventually come to pass. One recalls Pribislav Hippe from *The Magic Mountain* as an enigmatic young ephebe with whom the protagonist Hans Castorp is briefly infatuated, a figure who 'emerged imperceptibly out of the fog and into his life, slowly taking on clarity and palpability, until the moment when he was most near, most physically present, stood there in the foreground for a while, and then gradually receded and vanished again into the fog, without even the pain of farewell.'

Meanwhile, since the time is long, one can respond either with patience and quiet fortitude or, to keep oneself amused, with a provoking belligerence, as I have tried to do here. It is no doubt true, as the old adage has it, that one should not make so long a tale of the straw as of the corn, but where the straw is routinely regarded as the corn and the corn neglected for the straw, I see no option but to react with indignation and animus until the blessed time comes when the beneficiaries of the Great Disconnect pribislav from view. The thing to avoid is a bland pro-forma courtesy which tends to leave everything approximately where it initially was. As Herbert Leibowitz, editor of *Parnassus: Poetry in Review*, complains (vol. 25, nos. 1 and 2), 'Over the last fifteen years or so, as the prestige of high culture has steadily declined, the audience for belletristic criticism – as opposed to the jargon-riddled academic variety – has dwindled. Yet what I find perhaps even more distressing is the reluctance of poets to write honestly about their peers.' This is a course not without its perils and disruptions but it does have a respectable Etonian precedent, where it was called floccinaucinihilipilification.

I would like to conclude by focusing on a poem that I regard as a sort of emissary work, one accurately summarizing the present situation. I refer to George Gascoigne's little-known piece called 'Gascoigne's Woodmanship', addressed to Arthur, Lord Grey of Wilton, a patron of Edmund Spenser as well, on the occasion of a winter hunt on Grey's estate a little while after Gascoigne had returned to England from the Spanish campaigns. The poet professes bewilderment at his lack of success in the preference wars of the time, for although 'his heart be good, his hap is naught'. Whatever he attempts inevitably goes awry for reasons that he cannot fathom, at least initially. Basing his poem on the extended metaphor of archery, he complains that he 'shot sometimes to hit Philosophy', but missed the target. Next 'he shot to be a man of law' with the same result. He begins to suspect that he himself might be at fault for shooting 'the wronger way',

> Thinking the purse of prodigality
> Had been best mean to purchase such a prey ...

or that

... the flattering face which fleareth still
Had been full fraught with all fidelity,

an error of perception common among the naive and ingenuous. The list of
failures in his efforts to acquire favour and advantage continues until the
poet, in his frustration over the successes of the incompetents and 'crafty
courtiers' by whom he is surrounded in his own poetic and rhetorical field,
arrives at his peroration, wondering how it is that

> ... some that never handled such a bow
> Can hit the white, or touch it near the quick;
> Who can nor speak nor write in pleasant wise,
> Nor lead their life by Aristotle's rule,
> Nor argue well on questions that arise,
> Nor plead a case more than my Lord Mayor's mule.
> Yet they can hit the marks that I do miss,
> And win the mean which may the man maintain.

Perhaps, he goes on the speculate, the reason for his bad luck has to do,
finally, with his deep suspicion that should he hit the object of the hunt, for
example a doe emerging from the woods to stand directly before him, and if
he should strike her dead, she might 'prove a carrion carcass too'. In other
words, worldly success is just another illusion. What is more, as it occurs to
him on further reflection, its only justification is that it provides the
opportunity for sincere repentance at having overvalued it, especially if he is
the sort of man who is instinctively uneasy to 'content his greedy will / Under
the cloak of a contrary pretence.' For although the 'guileful marks' that attract
ambition may 'glister outwardly like gold', they are 'inwardly but brass, as
men may see' if only they scruple to look.

I think that worldly success would be quite nice and I suppose that most of
the good poets whose work I have canvassed would agree, but I am equally
convinced that the dedication to excellence and its occasional attainment is
far more desirable.[24] It would be ideal to enjoy both, of course – and possibly
one or two of my laudable candidates actually and improbably do – but in the
current slough of aesthetic and cultural achievement nothing can replace the
experience of authentic merit, whether immediately in the poet or vicariously
in the reader.

As for the poem we are examining here, it is far too witty and accomplished to be dismissed as an exercise in self-pity or as the crushing and vatting of sour grapes. In fact, as I intimated above, I have come to regard it as an exemplary document that addresses itself not only to the dilemma which confronted a somewhat baffled George Gascoigne but to all poets of whatever era who can speak or write in pleasant wise yet miss the guileful marks that others blindly hit. Gascoigne closes by ironically taking his poem down a notch, having told, 'God grant in season / A tedious tale in rime, but little reason.' The 'little reason', however, pertains not so much to the work we have just finished reading as to the times in which those poets who are incapable of the 'quaint conceit' are amply rewarded.

# Notes

1. Readers will remember Prostetnic Vogon Jeltz from Douglas Adams's *The Hitchhiker's Guide to the Galaxy*. The alien in question habitually tortures his victims by reciting his poetry to them while they are strapped in a chair. Death by prolonged suffering or summary execution generally follows.

2. Possibly we are already there. In the last twenty-five years or so, we have created a parodistic literary climate in which it would be more appropriate to award an annual prize to the worst poet in the country, because then at least the competition would be fierce, there would be no lack of candidates and no one could reasonably contest the results. We have now entered the world of pure slapstick. How else account for the fact that a poet like Fred Wah, author of arguably the most awful lines in all of Canadian poetry – lines, I hasten to add, that do not appear fortuitous or uncharacteristic – was honoured with a Governor General's Award and still enjoys considerable acclaim and influence. The lines in question, from 'Breathin' My Name with a Sigh': 'breathing somewhere / the air / as it comes out / ahead of me / "waahh, waahhh".' Another particular favourite of mine, courtesy of Western Canada's Lotus-land Express, is George Bowering's well-hung 'Inside the Tulip' where we read: 'Look at me long enough / and I will be a flower / or wet blackberries dangling / from a dripping bush ...' But a worst-lines competition would attract far too many worthy contestants to adjudicate in real time.

3. I might note here that the 'hieratic dispositions' to which I refer by no means rule out the rich deployment of a local or nonmetropolitan dialect, an idiom native to the place in which the poem is written or to the imagination in which it is engendered – consider, for example, the Alabama usage-and-syntax of Rodney Jones's work or Michael Lind's impressive Texan epic *The Alamo* or much of Derek Walcott whose phrases 'go be soaked in salt' and whose lines be drawn tight 'as ropes in this rigging'. But I do insist that this idiom must come to terms with the perennial, autonomous and 'transnational' form and medium of poetry itself, which, as Jonathan Culler has

observed, seems to have evolved in accordance with four determining princi-
ples: (1) intrinsic significance, (2) thematic unity, (3) metaphorical coherence,
and (4) formal resonance with the tradition, however remote or indirect or
inconspicuous. I would add a fifth element or principle which strikes me as a
*sine qua non*, namely, (5) memorable language, words annealed by seraphic
fire, or what Yeats called 'lyric cantillation', and Denis Donoghue 'words
revelling in shameless conjunction'. True poets and lovers of poetry have
always known that in poetry language comes before anything else. As Richard
Whately wrote in *Miscellaneous Remains* (1864), 'In prose, the language is the
vehicle for the matter; in poetry, the matter is the vehicle for the language.'

4. Lee's definitive essay is in many respects a brilliant and moving document but,
as a committed act of special pleading, it evinces an unfortunate over-the-top
infatuation with his subject that leads to the kind of unintentionally ridicu-
lous assertions I have excerpted within.

5. Some readers may feel it grossly unjust or invidious of me to invoke heavy-
weights like Yeats and Browning as standards of comparison. But that would
clinch my argument since Purdy and Ashbery – a.k.a. Reginald Bunthorne
and Archibald Grosvenor pursuing their Savoyard antics – have been and are
still being advertised as gargantuan presences in the world of poetry and
should thus be able to withstand assaying with the touchstone poets. That
they plainly do not should make us stop and reconsider and see that what is
happening in their poetry is really much ado about not much a-doing. (It is
only fair to add that Ashbery does make some kind of sense – although he
remains drab as ever – when he is quoted in someone else's poem, e.g., Mark
Strand's *Dark Harbor*, number xxviii.) But this ability to stop and reassess
would also require the kind of readers who, even if bemused by too much
wind, can still tell the difference between a dead leaf and a living butterfly.
Perhaps Ashbery's lacklustre lines in 'Strange Cinema' turn out to be oddly
appropriate to the state of poetry I am bemoaning (though what Ashbery is
bemoaning I suspect only Harold Bloom can tell):

> I shall petition the other board members
> but am afraid nothing will ever come right.
> It has been going on too long for this to happen ...

But these lines, of course, like practically the entire Ashbery oeuvre, are simply not poetry and have been going on too long for anything unprecedented or rejuvenating to happen. The last word should be given to Timothy Murphy who, in an interview in *The Cortland Review* for November 2001, dismisses Ashbery (along with A. R. Ammons) as 'frauds who hold their audiences in contempt'.

6. R. C. Jebb's *The Growth and Influence of Classical Greek Poetry*, published in 1893, is a text well worth consulting on matters of Greek prosody and, by extrapolation, its relation to our own customary practices and expectations. Other books on the subject that I have found useful and illuminating are the following: Jonathan Culler's *Structuralist Poetics* (whose classical citations I have followed), M. A. K. Halliday's *Short Introduction to Functional Grammar* and Yuri Lotman's *Analysis of the Poetic Text*.

7. This is also the gusty, emotive language of playwright Michel de Ghelderode's Jairus (in *Miss Jairus*): 'I am suffering so much, hoo!, and more, hoo!, and my flasks are going to spill over, hoo! Yet a beading tear must not be caught unawares in my right eye, hoo!, in my left eye, hoo! ...' For Jairus wishes to find 'soaring sentences, well-turned phrases, with an eternal meaning, that prop up the spirits'.

8. See 'The Trouble with Annie', where I take issue with the curfew sensibility that prevails in these parts. *Nunc dimittis*.

9. The twin paradigm for the elegiac subgenre we are considering is Dylan Thomas's 'Do Not Go Gentle' and Irving Layton's 'Keine Lazarovitch', golden poems, which are mutually unsurpassable. e. e. cummings' 'my father moved through dooms of love' perhaps makes a lesser third and Mary Oliver's 'Poem for My Father's Ghost' is a bright sparkle in this constellation of star performances.

10. The 2001 Governor General's Award jury, Erin Mouré, Lisa Robertson and John Steffler, described Clarke's winning entry, *Execution Poems*, as 'raging, gristly, public – and unflinchingly beautiful'. I find it quite impossible to agree – except maybe for the 'public' part – and would argue to the contrary that if one wants to demonstrate the lack of creative purchase and bite – and the

flaccid, almost *duodenal* thinking responsible for it in so much of our poetry –
one can't go wrong with Clarke. As Norm Sibum, the matching incompatible
I have chosen in text to contrast with Clarke, writes in 'Ordinary Time':

> Burn rosemary, cypress to purge the air.
> Festoon your house with fragrant branches.
> Light candles against the dark that is always with us.
> Do not flatter it …

11. This upscale and overpriced brand of ice cream is produced in New Jersey but
passed off for marketing purposes as exotically Danish. The trouble is, there is
no umlaut in Danish, just as there is no *poetry* in Bök.

12. Close attention to grammatical, syntactical and lexical details should not be
dismissed as trivial or picayune merely because we have no tradition of gram-
metric analysis in this country. Such details, as every accomplished poet
knows, are part of the fundamental groundwork of any poem. Each comma,
each article, each auxiliary, *every word*, is crucial to the overall economy of the
little heterocosm the poet is conjuring out of airy nothing.

With respect to diction, note for example how Timothy Steele – whom I've
had occasion to mention several times throughout this book – can take an
ugly-duckling word like 'swirled', which figures as half an entire line in the
Ondaatje piece, and swan it out with masterly panache:

> The wind dies, and the cloud Alps disappear,
>   And where the sun now sets, the sky's so swirled
> With smoky colors that the atmosphere
> Seems like the abstract beauty of the world.
>   – 'At Will Rogers Beach'

– where even the adjective 'abstract' concretely summarizes the concept of
abstraction in context. Or T. R. Hummer's image/anecdote of the boy falling
into a silo, 'oats / At the top swirling into a gold whirlpool,' with its internal
sonority and its perilous implication of what it is like to fall in love ('Where
You Go When She Sleeps').

13. The sources for the distinctions I am drawing are plentiful and various and

my citations are certainly far from exhaustive. For John Dennis, see his *Remarks on a Book Entitled Prince Arthur* (1696); for Alexander Pope, the Preface to his translation of *The Iliad* (1715); and for Thomas Gray, a letter of 1842 in the standard Gray's *Letters*. (Gray, anticipating Wilde, famously remarked that 'the language of the age is never the language of poetry.') What I call formulation (2) has, to the best of my knowledge, no single origin. The argument against rebarbatively common words was made perhaps most forcefully by John Dryden in the Dedication to his translation of *The Aeneid* (1697), where he dismissed them as 'Village-words [which] give us a mean Idea of the thing'; that against darkly obscure words, by Thomas Hobbes in a passage prefixed to *Homer's Odysses* (1675), where he advises against the 'Indiscretion' of using words that 'are not sufficiently known'. But as I intimated above, the literature on these topics is vast and unwieldy and my research is avowedly that of an interested amateur culling from years of jumbled note-taking, not that of a professional scholar.

In our own country today, the terms of this perennial distinction (and debate) have settled into a somewhat different idiom. The conflict is seen as that between 'the poetics of common sense' on the one side and 'innovative', 'verbovisual', or L=A=N=G=U=A=G=E (i.e., language-centred) poetry on the other. (See Bryan Sentes's essay, 'Bull Vaulting: A Plea for Alternatives in Canadian Poetry,' in *Matrix*, no. 58.) This distinction corresponds, albeit a little loosely, to the one I have drawn between written speech and encrypted prose. But what poets like Sentes or Christian Bök (whom Sentes cites but also critiques) perceive as an agon between competing schools or practices, I regard as a family relationship between quarrelling twins.

14. Laurence Lerner puts the matter succinctly – and fairly – in his *Introduction to English Poetry* where he addresses the 'pococurante reader' (cf. *Candide*) in an effort to revive the dormant awareness of the importance of both living tradition and innovative language. 'There is a pleasure in listening to the rhythms of actual speech, but it is not a specifically literary pleasure, and those modern poets who write in pure speech rhythms

> – we finished clearing the last
> Section of trail by noon,
> High on the ridge-side
> Two thousand feet above the creek –

offer us the pleasure of recognizing the genuine but in the end are behaving more like tape-recorders than poets.' These observations were made in 1975, but nothing much seems to have changed since then.

15. To denote the opposite of 'irre-factant', Bohm coins from the Greek the term 'rheomode' to suggest the emphasis on flowing/manifesting. The idea is similar to J. L. Austin's more famous concept of 'performative' words developed in the seminal *How to Do Things with Words*, although the latter placed the emphasis on their oral and instantaneous aspects. Performatives derive from what Austin calls Rule A. 1: 'There must exist an accepted conventional procedure having a certain conventional effect, that procedure to include the uttering of certain words by certain persons in certain places,' that is, words that denote such actions as betting, promising, marrying, etc., words that do what they say. Performatives produce reality rather than merely represent it and are thus not true or false but felicitous or infelicitous, which is clearly a poetic consideration as well. Yet, strangely enough, Austin does not recognize literary language as performative, for he believed that in literary language illocution disappears (illocutionary force signifies the *participation* of language in what it signifies) and only locutions (semantic units) are left which are, moreover, generally inapplicable to experience. Thus he famously condemned literature as 'parasitic upon its [language's] normal use', as 'not serious'. For example, a phrase like Donne's 'Go and catch a falling star' suspends the 'normal conditions of reference' since it implies that the imperative can somehow be executed. Using his philosophical lexicon, he would say that literary language has no 'perlocutionary' effect, the latter term referring to consequences in the real world.

Notwithstanding, literary and especially poetic language would seem to me to form one of the optimum cases of performative or illocutionary felicity and indeed that may well be its defining characteristic. Richard Ohmann probably clinches the case for literary illocution in an essay entitled 'Speech Acts and the Definition of Literature' in which he develops the subtle and forceful argument of 'purported imitation', of literature as a 'quasi-speech act'. The idea – which I regard as undeniable – is that readers build their fictional (or poetic) worlds by imagining which of that world's communal rules or conventions of affect and response would permit speech, as represented in or by the text, to behave in a purportedly constructive way. In other words, we are capable of creating and believing in imaginary worlds where speech can do *what the novel or the poem represents it as doing or as being able to do.* And this can plainly lead to changes for good or bad in the real world as well. Consider the Homeric texts as applied to civic life by Solon or the effect of Goethe's *Werther* on an entire generation – texts which came to have the force of law whether institutional or unofficial. For a brief but helpful tour of these issues, see Sandy Petrey, *Speech Acts and Literary Theory,* a book that served to confirm my own reading and thinking on the subject and directed me to the Ohmann essay, with which I was unfamiliar.

16. As C. S. Peirce says of the various 'phanerons' of the world, i.e., the blended phenomena which are present to the mind, 'they are so inextricably mixed together that no one can be isolated, yet it is manifest that their characters are quite disparate.' Common language and poetic diction are precisely such phanerons: composite totalities that mingle inextricably with one another and are yet in their essential natures absolutely distinct. A trace of Peircean 'phaneroscopy' helps to keep us as poets scrupulous about what we do and aware that the oral dictionary and the poetic glossary coincide at innumerable points but are only approximately coterminous.

17. The case was conclusively made long ago in Geoffrey of Vinsauf's medieval rhetoric, *Poetria nova,* which, despite its heavy pedagogical tone, set the terms of our centuries-long discourse on the subject.

> *Si quis habet fundare domum, non currit ad actum*
> *Impetuosa manus: intrinseca linea cordis*
> *Praemetitur opus, seriemque sub ordine certo*
> *Interior praescribit homo …*

> ['If one sets out to build a house he does not rush to work
> with impetuous hand; instead the heart's intrinsic plumb-line
> first measures out the work and the inner man plans the steps
> in a particular order …']

This is not really so different from Jeanette Winterson's notion, in *Sexing the Cherry,* of the genuine artist's ability, learned or innate, 'to make the foreground into the background, so that the distractions of the everyday no longer take up our energy.' Adopting a term from science, she calls this unique capacity 'superconductivity', which she understands as 'a criterion for true art, as opposed to cunning counterfeit'. Whether we see it as a 'house' that we wish to build (Vinsauf) or 'this other different place' from which nuisances and aberrations are banished (Winterson), the fact remains that '[w]hen we are drawn into the art we are drawn out of ourselves' and into the realm of structure, coherence, and purpose. In this way, as I have contended throughout, we are also drawn to reconnect with a sustaining and historically validated human source long abrogated and forgotten.

18. See Virgil's third Eclogue:

> *Qui Bauium non odit, amet tua carmina, Maeui,*
> *atque idem iungat uulpes et mulgeat hircos.*

> [Let him who hates not Bavius love Maevius' songs,
> And likewise let him milk he-goats and yoke the fox.]

Whether we are dealing with the vulgar Bavius or the egghead Maevius, who represent the two major poetic schools I have been excoriating that compose in either speech or cipher, we should strike them equally from our contact list.

19. This is even truer of the constituent lexicality of such literary production, whose value is usually nil or pretty close to it. As on our restaurant bills, the dinbartle is generally out of all proportion to the bever.

20. Another way of accounting for this 'bad decision' is to put it down to a fundamental *insincerity* in the motivation of these poets; in other words, it is the display of self and not devotion to the work that seems to operate as a primary intent. This is especially true of the two major centres for poetry on the continent, New York and Toronto, despite the superficial differences. New York glitz or Toronto grunge – they amount to the same thing, a poetry that connects with nothing of abiding significance or common concern. As Greek poet Nadina Dimitriou writes in 'Snap-Shots 1', 'The Insignificant causes the rift / and insincerity is its reason.'

21. Only if poet and reader meet on the level of mutual respect and consideration can we expect to find what Wordsworth in the preface to the 1814

*Excursion* called, in a different yet analogous context, 'the spousal verse / Of this great consummation'. Similarly, what Sir Joshua Reynolds in his *Eleventh Discourse* recommended for the landscape painter of his time applies equally to the poet of our own: to work 'not for the virtuoso or the naturalist but for the common observer of life and nature'. We ignore this advice at our peril. As Elaine Scarry puts it in her provocative *The Body in Pain* in the chapter where she is discussing the ways in which the reciprocation of the artifact should exceed its initial projection, 'the poet projects the private acuities of sentience into the sharable, because objectified, poem, which exists not for its own sake but to be read: its power now moves back from the object realm to the human realm where sentience itself is remade.' The poet, then, is working to complete the arc of creation by *connecting* the moment of the original projection of the object out into the artifactual world with its *generalized* human source and in this way 'to remake human sentience; by means of the poem, he or she enters into and in some way alters the alive percipience of other persons.' To rephrase the issue we have been tackling in Scarry's language, the bulk of contemporary poetry is mainly projection accompanied by little or no reciprocation.

22. We can always hope their time will soon be done although the prognosis is not encouraging. How long will this interregnum last? Applying to the object of our study the 'Copernican' equations (i.e., our terrestrial vantage point is in no way unique) of Princeton astrophysicist J. Richard Gott III, we will make three prior assumptions for our approximative purposes: that Canadian poetry began circa 1750 (Thomas Cary and J. Mackay wrote a few years later but 1750 seems a tidy starting point), that our object is a relatively unitary or coherent phenomenon and thus susceptible to observation, and that *we are presently not in a particularly special place from which to carry out our observations*. With regard to the Copernican postulate, we expect $t_{now}$ will be located randomly in the interval between $t_{begin}$ and $t_{end}$. By dividing ($t_{now}$-$t_{begin}$) by ($t_{end}$-$t_{begin}$), we produce a random number ($r_1$) uniformly distributed between 0 and 1 with a probability P=0.95 (the so-called 'confidence level' that pollsters designate as '19 times out of 20') that the fraction ($r_1$) will be between 0.025 and 0.975, and that 50 per cent of the time it will fall between 0.25 and 0.75. Working with the latter set of figures to simplify the issue: if we suppose, as is likely, that we are somewhere in the middle two

quarters of the history of Canadian poetry – a nonspecial place sufficiently Copernican for our calculations – it follows that either 1/4 or 3/4 of its actual history has passed. In the first case, the future is three times as long as the past; in the second, three quarters of its lifespan have already passed. Thus, if we posit that Canadian poetry is 252 years old (i.e., 2002-1750) there is at least a 50 per cent chance that our poetry's future duration will settle in the range between an upper limit of 756 years and a lower limit of 84 years. But a best case scenario of 84 years is still, Gott help us, rather depressing. Of course, in deploying the second hypothesis, we know that Canadian poetry has a 25 per cent possibility of malingering somewhere in the first or the last quarter of its lifetime, which would give us either more than 756 or less than 84 years respectively, but we cannot extract more precise figures from this murkier state of affairs. However, with respect to the first hypothesis, if by some uncomputable miracle it so happens that .975 of its history has already passed, then an elementary calculation tells us that Canadian poetry as presently constituted will reach its terminus in only 6.46 years, which would give some of us an opportunity to rejoice. But since the latter possibility is remote, this would give some of us even more reason to lament. And yet we might note that Gott's derivations obviously work best for expanding populations but also suggest that in cases of exponential growth there is always a significant chance of an imminent or sudden decline. Since Canadian poetry is ramifying without let or hindrance, hope once again revives.

23. With respect to this point, anthropologist Grant McCracken formulates the idea with aphoristic nicety in his study of cultural speciation and difference, *Plenitude*, as follows: 'Thus does tradition play midwife to novelty.' Mary Kinzie takes it as a 'threshold assumption' in a particularly acute passage in her *A Poet's Guide to Poetry* that 'most poetry is the product of experiments on the past, acts of recombining already invented substances in such a way that they are transformed.' We might think of this process as the poetic equivalent of alternative splicing, the reshuffling of genomic sequences to yield new information.

24. Although I must say that I am extremely suspicious of the kind of worldly success enjoyed by hucksters like the Dove-Viebahns boasting about participating in every imaginable poetry festival and waltzing on the parquet of the Executive Mansion. How good, how consoling to learn that poetry really

matters and that a will-o'-the-wisp like Rita Dove enjoys conversations with Meryl Streep about children, landfills, poetry and movies. (See *Fred's Annual Letter*, no. 12, Summer 2001.)

# Acknowledgements

SOME OF THESE PIECES, generally in abridged form, others subsequently revised, have appeared elsewhere as follows: 'The Flight from Canada' in *CV II*, reprinted in 'The Insecurity of Art: Essays on Poetics'; 'Acorn, Lemm and Ojibway', 'The Trouble with Annie', 'Double Exile and Montreal English-Language Poetry', 'Peter Van Toorn' and 'The Colour of Literature' in *Books in Canada*; 'Louis Dudek: A Personal Memoir' in *Quill & Quire*; 'Pliny's Villa' (originally entitled 'On Modern Poetry'), 'Reading Richard Outram' and 'Standard Average Canadian' in *Canadian Notes & Queries*; 'Reflections on the Laureateship', 'Dougie's Angels' and variant recensions of 'Standard Average Canadian' and 'The Colour of Literature' in the *National Post*; 'Ardour Illuminates' in *The Sewanee Review*; 'An Open Letter to Lorna Crozier' in the *Montreal Gazette*; and 'The Montreal Forties' in the *Montreal Review of Books*.

David Solway is the author of many books of poetry including the award-winning *Modern Marriage*, as well as *Bedrock, Chess Pieces, Saracen Island: The Poetry of Andreas Karavis* and *The Lover's Progress: Poems after William Hogarth*, the latter illustrated by Marion Wagschal and adapted for the stage by Curtain Razors. His work has been anthologized in *The Penguin Book of Canadian Verse*, McClelland and Stewart's *New Canadian Poetry, Border Lines: Contemporary Poetry in English* from Copp Clark, and *The Bedford Introduction to Literature* from St. Martin's Press. Among his prose publications, *Education Lost* won the QSPELL Prize for Nonfiction and *Random Walks* was a finalist for *Le Grand Prix du Livre de Montréal*. His most recent prose work, *The Turtle Hypodermic of Sickenpods*, was released by McGill-Queen's in 2001. Solway publishes regularly in such journals as *The Atlantic Monthly, The Sewanee Review, Books in Canada* and *Canadian Notes & Queries*, and is an occasional contributor to the book pages of the *National Post*. His more specialized writings have appeared in the *International Journal of Applied Semiotics, Policy Options: Institute on Research in Public Policy*, and the *Journal of Modern Greek Studies*. Solway has recently completed a new collection of poems entitled *Franklin's Passage*, forthcoming with McGill-Queen's in fall, 2003, and is now working on his fourth book in education and culture, entitled *Reading, Riting and Rhythmitic*. He was appointed writer-in-residence at Concordia University for 1999-2000 and is currently a contributing editor with *Canadian Notes & Queries* and an associate editor with *Books in Canada*.